Musical Development

*Or, Remarks on the Spirit
of the Principal Music Forms*

Joseph Goddard

CAMBRIDGE UNIVERSITY PRESS

Cambridge, New York, Melbourne, Madrid, Cape Town,
Singapore, São Paolo, Delhi, Tokyo, Mexico City

Published in the United States of America by Cambridge University Press, New York

www.cambridge.org
Information on this title: www.cambridge.org/9781108038614

© in this compilation Cambridge University Press 2011

This edition first published 1868
This digitally printed version 2011

ISBN 978-1-108-03861-4 Paperback

This book reproduces the text of the original edition. The content and language reflect the beliefs, practices and terminology of their time, and have not been updated.

Cambridge University Press wishes to make clear that the book, unless originally published by Cambridge, is not being republished by, in association or collaboration with, or with the endorsement or approval of, the original publisher or its successors in title.

CAMBRIDGE LIBRARY COLLECTION

Books of enduring scholarly value

Music

The systematic academic study of music gave rise to works of description, analysis and criticism, by composers and performers, philosophers and anthropologists, historians and teachers, and by a new kind of scholar - the musicologist. This series makes available a range of significant works encompassing all aspects of the developing discipline.

Musical Development

Joseph Goddard (1833–1910) was a philosopher, theorist and historian of the music of the late eighteenth and early nineteenth centuries, who developed some highly influential ideas about the relationship between music and human evolution. First published in 1868, this study presents Goddard's theory on the connection between music and the human spirit, in which he argues that two major counterparts of emotion – instinctive and abstract – correlate directly with two key elements of music: melody and harmony. He demonstrates this through a fascinating and thorough comparative analysis of the works of Mozart, Beethoven, Haydn and Mendelssohn, and moves on to show how emotion is expressed in the melodic and harmonic styles of sacred music and opera. Concluding with a detailed analysis of how mental progress has influenced the development of music, this thorough and judicious work remains of interest in the fields of music history, philosophy, and theory.

Cambridge University Press has long been a pioneer in the reissuing of out-of-print titles from its own backlist, producing digital reprints of books that are still sought after by scholars and students but could not be reprinted economically using traditional technology. The Cambridge Library Collection extends this activity to a wider range of books which are still of importance to researchers and professionals, either for the source material they contain, or as landmarks in the history of their academic discipline.

Drawing from the world-renowned collections in the Cambridge University Library, and guided by the advice of experts in each subject area, Cambridge University Press is using state-of-the-art scanning machines in its own Printing House to capture the content of each book selected for inclusion. The files are processed to give a consistently clear, crisp image, and the books finished to the high quality standard for which the Press is recognised around the world. The latest print-on-demand technology ensures that the books will remain available indefinitely, and that orders for single or multiple copies can quickly be supplied.

The Cambridge Library Collection will bring back to life books of enduring scholarly value (including out-of-copyright works originally issued by other publishers) across a wide range of disciplines in the humanities and social sciences and in science and technology.

MUSICAL DEVELOPMENT.

MUSICAL DEVELOPMENT;

OR,

REMARKS ON THE SPIRIT

OF

THE PRINCIPAL MUSICAL FORMS.

BY

JOSEPH GODDARD,

AUTHOR OF 'THE PHILOSOPHY OF MUSIC.'

LONDON:
THOMAS MURBY, 32, BOUVERIE STREET,
FLEET STREET, E.C.;
SIMPKIN, MARSHALL & CO., STATIONERS' HALL COURT, E.C.

[ALL RIGHTS RESERVED.]

LONDON :
PRINTED BY WARREN HALL AND CO.,
CAMDEN ROAD, N.W.

PREFACE.

THIS work does not treat either of the history or of the technicalities of music. Several years ago the question used frequently to suggest itself to the present writer whilst listening to fine music, whether its strong and elevating influence might not be explained. Looking for indications of music in nature,—i. e. not only for musical sounds, which are abundant enough, but for musical expression also,—he concluded that the effects of tone and accent in speech, are such indications; and he was first led to this conclusion not by the palpable resemblance of modulation in speech and melody, but by experiencing that the inward sensation produced by the eloquent enunciation of important language, greatly resembles that produced by such music as Handel's choruses, the expression of which depends so much upon the principle of rhythm. Hence he first assumed that emphasis and phrase in language are rudimentary effects of rhythm and phrase in music;* and afterwards concluded that the former effects, together with modulation, are animated by an impulse of the same order as that which gives rise to music. He expressed these views some time back in a work, a new

---

* It is perhaps unnecessary to say that these different terms, emphasis, rhythm, phrase, do not refer to effects of different natures, but to different forms of one principle, both rhythm and phrase being certain arrangements of the effect of emphasis.

edition of which he hopes soon to publish, entitled 'The Philosophy of Music.'

This being so, he has thought that observation of the spirit in which the above effects relative to language are prompted, might throw light upon the spirit in which music is prompted. A digest of the results of this observation, and the residuum of the passing ideas the subject has suggested, constitute the present work.

The author acknowledges with much pleasure, expressions of sympathy received during the progress of the work, from Mr. William Chappell, Mr. J. F. Duggan, Dr. Rimbault, Mr. Charles Salaman, Mr. J. W. Davison, Mr. J. Goss, Mr. J. Ella, The Rev. E. Young, Miss Emily Ham, Mr. J. Fulcher (Glasgow), Mr. J. Smyth (B. M. Royal Art.), and Mr. Thomas Murby, amongst others; and is further desirous of acknowledging his indebtedness to the last named gentleman for his very able and careful assistance in the revision of the proof-sheets. He has only further to add, that the sympathy here acknowledged, is sympathy with the investigation of music; and that it was given in ignorance of the particular opinions and ideas expressed or implied in the following pages.

136, ST. PAUL'S ROAD,
CAMDEN SQUARE, N.W.

CONTENTS.

CHAPTER I.
THE TWO CHARACTERS OF SENTIMENT, AND THE TWO SECTIONS OF MUSICAL EFFECT 9

CHAPTER II.
THE EXIGENCY IN EXPRESSION WHICH ABSTRACT SENTIMENT INVOLVES, AND THE STRUCTURAL PLAN OF THE GREAT MODERN INSTRUMENTAL FORMS OF COMPOSITION 26

CHAPTER III.
A COMPARATIVE ANALYSIS OF THE SPIRIT OF THE INSTRUMENTAL MUSIC OF HAYDN, MOZART, BEETHOVEN, AND MENDELSSOHN.. 44

CHAPTER IV.
THE INTELLECTUAL POSITION OF INSTRUMENTAL MUSIC 74

CHAPTER V.
THE PRINCIPLES ON WHICH THE MUSICAL AND LITERARY PLAN OF AN OPERA, SHOULD BE BASED 83

CHAPTER VI.
THE SPIRIT OF SACRED MUSIC.—REMARKS ON THE ORATORIO 120

CHAPTER VII.
SOME REMARKS CONCERNING THE INFLUENCE OF MENTAL PROGRESS UPON MUSIC.—CONCLUSION 137

MUSICAL DEVELOPMENT.

CHAPTER I.

THE TWO CHARACTERS OF SENTIMENT, AND THE TWO SECTIONS OF MUSICAL EFFECT.

HUMAN emotion, regarded comprehensively, is seen to be of two general orders: the feeling we bear to one another, which arises through our human relations, being one; and that which is not elicited through social intercourse, but which we possess solely with reference to our own minds and to nature generally, being the other. The former is personal or instinctive, the latter mental or abstract, emotion; one is common feeling, the other, though still broad, exceptional. The first order of sentiment is involved in that vast sympathy which obeys Shakespear's 'touch of nature;' the second may be described as that 'pure passion' alluded to by the poet where he says—

> 'I become
> Portion of that around me, and to me
> High mountains are a feeling.' * * *

Musical effect is well known to consist materially of two distinctive elements, both composed of sounds arranged in certain successions, the principle of arrangement being in the one case variation of pitch, in the other, variation of force. One principle is predominant in music of a character suggested by the term, melody; the other, in music whose characteristic is a more or less elaborate accentuation: harmony is common to, and deepens and enhances, both sections of musical effect. I shall now endeavour to demonstrate that the two characters of human emotion on the one hand, and of musical effect on the other, have a direct relation; to show that the melodic style of music is naturally and peculiarly appropriate for expressing the instinctive type of feeling, and that the marked rhythmic style is in the same degree appropriate for expressing feeling of the more abstract type.*

This proposition regarded absolutely, may not appear at first sight, practically important. The considerations, however, that the process of its establishment gives rise to, will enable us to unfold the moral theory of the art of music. And the natural principle involved in this sympathetic divergence in the character of emotion, and in the form of musical

---

* By music of a marked rhythmic style, I mean music where the variation in effect,—and therefore where the expression and character,—lies mainly in the rhythm. Music exemplifies the principle of rhythm in two general forms, and for two objects; in a regularly measured form, and for a mechanical purpose, and in a variable and broader form, and for a poetical purpose. The measured accentuation,—the time,—of a piece of music, may be most strongly marked and yet this accentuation may be the furthest removed feature in the effect from the characteristic features of the individual composition. In the case of *dance music*, to give an instance, the majority of pieces in each form of this kind of composition, would be indistinguishable but for the difference of their *melodies*. It is obvious that as regards rhythm, there is here little or no variation of effect. On the other hand, composition where the characteristic design is worked mainly out of the principle of rhythm, involves an order of music which includes such works as Handel's choruses. There are compositions of this order, in which the measured and invariable accentuation is subdued, where there is no melody, where the harmonic changes are both rare and of the simplest nature, where the whole character and individuality lies in the shaping and grouping of its larger rhythmic features, and of which the effect is most impressive and sublime.

effect, is serviceable as an implement for interpreting the spirit and meaning of all the important musical styles: among these, of that abstract-instrumental style which has attained such full development in the works of Beethoven.

In entering upon the consideration of the proposition under notice, it is necessary, preparatively, to refer to the following facts;—as man's crowning inward endowment is the high degree in which he possesses the phenomenon, mind, so that which most elevates and distinguishes him with regard to external qualities, is the power through which mind manifests itself, or his faculty of demonstration: the main issue of human demonstrativeness, is language; its higher channel, fine art.

In the living action of language work the three grand principles through which human demonstration is consummated, whereby all ideas of material things are communicated, and all moral sensations expressed. The simplest is that which we shall term the principle of *symbolical association*—of raising ideas in others by the use of a regular machinery of suggestion. Certain sounds, or words, are associated with certain distinctly defined ideas—ideas of objects, persons, actions, qualities, conditions, or sensations; and a particular succession of words being uttered, a correlative train of ideas is at once suggested. The process is mechanical, *i.e.* the mind receives impressions thus communicated, whilst in a passive condition—without special exertion. It is to be observed, this principle of expression only embraces emotions of distinctly-defined character, and which are common to human experience; its name implies thus much, as the influence of association is the resuscitation of old impressions. It is also to be noticed that it does not afford exhaustive expression to feeling, or arouse deep sympathy, but serves mainly to suggest the idea of feeling.

Another of these three principles of demonstration is, that of *representation* or *imitation*,—the expressing and conveying impressions by reproducing in full extent and detail the original incitation of those impressions. This is the psychological principle of the arts of painting, sculpture, and the drama; and it prevails extensively in poetry, and amidst graphic descriptive passages in ordinary language.

It is to be observed, this principle embraces sentiment too special and complex to be communicable by the power of association; that it affords scope for lengthened expression, and arouses a vivid sympathy.

There is thirdly, the principle of *direct expression*,— the conveying a particular temper of feeling through the effect of the modulation and accentuation of the voice. This principle enters largely into all rhetorical effects in ordinary speech, into all sentential and metrical effects in the higher forms of language, and into poetry; it prevails wholly in the effect of music.

All these principles may be remarked conjointly operating in language. Thus, in the instance of a speaker making a communication involving both fact and feeling, we find that in the literal portion of the communication—in the expression of simple ideas and generic sentiment, the principle of *symbolical association* operates; whilst in the descriptive passages—in the graphic delineation of scene, character, and circumstance—in the full reproduction of certain influences in nature or life, the principle of *representation*—of painting, sculpture, and the drama, prevails; but in that portion of the communication where the sentiment being expressed is most original— where it is peculiar to the conceiver alone,—in the delicate modulation of the voice, and the dexterous moulding of the phrase, the remarkable principle of *direct expression*—of poetry and music, is in action.

It may favour the attainment of a distinct idea of each of these principles, if I briefly recapitulate that the first mentioned, acts upon the mind chiefly through the process of *association*, the second, through the process of *representation*, and the other, by effects which are purely *phonetic*.

It is with the last principle that we have chiefly to do in these considerations. I have to direct the reader's particular attention to the fact that language has besides its more mechanical and circuitous forms of action, another action which works in the effect of different degrees of inflection of the voice, and by a more or less marked and variedly arranged accentuation. It is to be observed that this action is of a peculiarly direct character, *i.e.*, in working impressiveness, it does not, like language in its other actions, refer to ideas and feelings already in the mind of a listener, or to effects without; it operates conjointly with those processes, but in so far as it is itself concerned, it involves no intermediate process whatever: it has, it would seem, the property of imbuing feeling spontaneously, and hence I term it the principle of *direct expression*.

The function of this principle appears to be, to express and convey that moral impressure which is most original, which is, in the first place, peculiar to the conceiver alone. Where, for instance, in ordinary speech, ideas mechanically suggested, are modified or enlarged by effects of modulation and accentuation; or where, in the higher forms of language, description is enhanced by sentential design or metrical effect,—the property of the action in question, is, to superadd to the more stereotyped emotion conjured up by other means of demonstration, the expression of a further and finer phase of feeling peculiar to the speaker alone.* At the same time it is observable

---

* Dr. Blair, speaking of the art of rightly using the effect of *emphasis*, in 'delivery,' says:—' It is one of the greatest trials of a true and just taste; and must arise from feeling delicately ourselves, and from judging accurately of what is fittest to strike the feelings of others.' *Lectures on Rhetoric, &c.*

that where in speech modulation and accentuation imbue a particular phase of moral impressure, they also imbue a sense of the general emotion involved; that they act broadly as well as particularly, just as the human countenance whilst wearing a particular expression, wears also a general one.*

* Long after the above text was written I met with the following allusion to the subject of these observations, and I quote it as evidence that modulation and accentuation are beginning to be regarded as an important element in language, and as worthy of deeper and more exclusive investigation than has been hitherto given them. Sir Edward Lytton Bulwer in 'Caxtoniana' remarks:—' In every good prose-writer there will be found a certain harmony of sentence, which cannot be displaced without injury to his meaning. His own ear has accustomed itself to regular measurements of time to which his thoughts learn mechanically to regulate their march. And in prose as in verse *it is the pause, be it long or short, which the mind is compelled to make, in order to accommodate its utterance to the ear, that serves to the completer formation of the ideas conveyed.* * * * * For reasons of its own prose has therefore a rhythm of its own. But by rhythm I do not mean the monotonous rise and fall of balanced periods, nor the amplification of needless epithets, in order to close the sentence with a Johnsonian chime. Every style has its appropriate music; but without a music of some kind it is not style—it is scribbling. And even when we take those writers of the last century in whom the taste of the present condemns an over elaborate care for sound, we shall find that the sense which they desire to express, so far from being sacrificed to sound, is rendered with singular distinctness; a merit which may be reasonably ascribed, in great part, to the increased attention with which the mind revolves its ideas in its effort to harmonise their utterance.' It does not appear to have struck the writer of the above, that the 'music of prose' is part of the general expression, and, in itself, both expresses

It will have been remarked that in describing this principle as the influence operating in the modulation and accentuation of the voice I refer to it as working in two different forms :—in the different relations of sounds as regards pitch, and as regards force. To thoroughly pursue the consideration of

and conveys a portion of the ideas involved,—that it thus has a distinct and direct function; although he is very near this idea in the passage which I have distinguished by italics. In the mind ' accommodating its utterance to the ear,' and, 'harmonising its utterance,' there must be more involved than simply the instinct to please the ear. For the great power which this 'music of prose' possesses to aid both expression and perception, cannot depend upon the sole fact that the ear demands to be pleased with the form of the mind's utterance. The ear, like the eye, is a sense calculated for fulfilling a finer office than that of carrying on a process of symbolical association; viz., the office of conducting to the consciousness the subtler species of outward effect: and thus it is an organ of the higher portion of the mind's language. A writer in adapting a passage to his ear is adding to it a burden for the finer perceptions of his readers. Instead, therefore, of the fulness which the music of prose gives to expression, being,—as Sir Lytton Bulwer implies,—caused indirectly, through the increased attention with which the mind revolves its ideas in order to harmonise their utterance, it is caused directly, by the harmony itself; it is this harmony which completes the mind's utterance, which expresses that within the mind which mere words leave unexpressed, which strikes an appreciative sense in the listener, that words alone could not reach. Music in language is not an accidental feature, indirectly beneficial; it is a principle of expression.

Since writing the foregoing note, I find the substance of the statement with which it concludes, has been remarked by Sheridan. The reader will further observe, there is another coincidence involved between this principle of direct expression, it is necessary to examine it not only in speech but throughout, and even beyond, the whole area of expression occupied by language; from simple modulation and accentuation in ordinary speech, past the broader and more elaborate forms of these effects in rhetoric, their artistic shapes in poetry, to their highest development and wholly emancipated action in music. Such an examination will, I believe, impress the mind mainly with three facts,—the first two referring to material, and the last, to moral circumstances,—which attend the principle of direct expression in the forms of demonstration

this work and the following quotation. In the portion of the latter which I have distinguished by italics, the same classification of Emotion is implied, that I have made in regarding it as of the two general orders, *instinctive*, and *abstract*.

'All that passes in the mind of man may be reduced to two classes, which I call Ideas and Emotions. By Ideas I mean all thoughts which rise and pass in succession through the mind. By Emotions, all exertions of the mind in arranging, combining, and separating its ideas; *as well as all the effects produced on the mind itself by those ideas, from the more violent agitation of the passions, to the calmer feelings produced by the operation of the intellect and the fancy.* In short, thought is the object of the one, internal feeling, of the other. That which serves to express the former, I call the Language of Ideas; and the latter, the Language of Emotions. Words are the signs of the one, Tones, of the other. Without the use of these two sorts of language, it is impossible to communicate through the ear all that passes in the mind of man.'

Sheridan on the Art of Reading.

it traverses. The first truth is, that modulation and inflection in speech are embryo effects of the principle of melody in music; the second is, that accentuation in speech is of the same nature as rhythm in music;* and the third is, that throughout colloquial speech, oratory, and poetry, the more or less elaborate employments of this principle of modulation and accentuation, inevitably occur as the truths and sentiments expressed, more or less ascend in character. It is, in fact, obvious that whilst modulation and accentuation in ordinary speech mostly enwrap incidental truth and instinctive personal sentiment, their more conspicuous presence in oratory, and their elaborate and systematised enunciation in poetry, are mainly the echo of broader truth and of that order of sentiment which arises through mental exercise.

* It is not implied that the two elements of music have become developed from the two elements of direct expression in language, but that they belong respectively to the same principles of demonstration. It is assumed that those peculiarities in the constitution of man that cause certain effects of modulation and accentuation in language, to both express and imbue certain emotions, are the main inward conditions that render him susceptible to the impulse and emotional influence of music. These occult faculties combined with a portion of that capacity for pleasure we possess in the cultivated exercise of the higher senses, may be said to compose the natural foundation of musical appreciation.

The last of these facts involves, moreover, this striking peculiarity;—in the degree that the matter of a statement rises in character, and,—by consequence,—assumes elaborate expressional form, so does such form become more exclusively composed of the rhythmic element of effect, and depend less upon the tonal element. It is apparent even from a passing consideration, that in rhetoric and poetry, the eloquence—the impressiveness resulting from manner of expression, is produced almost solely by variety of accentuation, by rhythmical design; whilst the pure vocal tone,—supposing the expression be uttered,—becomes firmer and steadier, and loses almost altogether the sharp inflection and the tender modulation indigenous to the language of ordinary speech.* It will be found in the case of an orator, that wherever his discourse embraces the instinctive sentiments of the heart, his tone becomes more delicate and changeable; whilst, where his language is animated by

---

* A contradiction to this fact seems to present itself in the case of the drama; but it immediately disappears before the consideration that the general circumstances of the drama are those of life, and that the language of the drama is thus to a large extent, of the character of the language of ordinary life.

feeling of a more abstract kind, such as that aroused by broad truth, his phrasing becomes more massive and elaborate, and his tone steadier and more monotonous. Now these considerations;—that where in language the truth involved is mainly broad and ideal, and the sentiment of the abstract type, the principle of direct expression assumes forms more elaborate and defined than anywhere else; and that in the degree that the above occurs, such forms are more largely composed of the element of accentuation alone;—point to the inference that mental sentiment has a natural tendency to unfold in its expression, rhythmic effect. Whilst the consideration that personal feeling is mainly couched in language where effects of modulation are more exclusively conspicuous, points to the conclusion that the instinctive type of feeling has a natural tendency in being expressed, to unfold tonal effect. Independently of analogy, it is apparent from ordinary consideration of the action of language, that this is really the case; that it is the tone, the modulation, that flies, like a spark, from the warmth of personal feeling, instinctive sentiment, ordinary human emotion; and that the broader sympathy is indicated by the sentential effect, the strongly defined accentuation : that the variations of tonal pitch denote the personal sentiment in a communication, whilst abstract emotion is denoted by rhythmical change.

The fact is transparent that such instinctive personal sentiments as love, solicitude, grief, betray themselves principally in the tone, the delicate modulation of the voice, whilst such abstract sentiments as reverence, admiration, patriotism,—sentiments rising out of broad ideas, as of Providence, goodness, liberty, justice,—principally demonstrate themselves in effects of accentuation—in the marked emphasis and pause— in sentential design. There is thus *a priori* argument for anticipating that the natural characteristic features of music, inspired by sentiment of the instinctive and abstract types respectively, will be melodic outline on the one hand, and rhythmic outline on the other. As melody is of the same nature as intonation in speech, effects whereof personal feeling has a natural tendency to dictate, it is reasonable to assume that a melodious style of music is naturally favorable for expressing feeling of this nature. And as all rhythmic effect in music is of the same nature as phrase in speech, effects of which emotion of an abstract nature has a natural tendency to dictate, it is reasonable to conclude that a musical style possessing bold rhythmic outline,—such as that involved in orchestral and choral works,—is naturally favorable for expressing emotion of the abstract order.

I have, thus far, made one grand division in the spirit of musical style. Two distinctive prevailing forms being perceptible in the outward plan of all musical effect,—the sinuous or melodic on the one hand, and the conspicuously accentuated on the other,—from probing the moral circumstances out of which the rudiments of these forms arise in language, it is assumed that the one is the naturally appropriate general form for music originating in the impulse of natural feeling, the other the naturally appropriate general form for music having its inspiration in abstract sentiment. And this assumption is based on the facts that in all human intercommunication, the moral element underlying it tends naturally to indicate itself in these two ways :—the personal and instinctive emotion, in the tonal change, the mental sentiment—the more abstract emotion, in variety of accentuation.*

It is thus assumed that the same demonstrative instinct man unfolds in language, he betrays in music.

* This general proposition stated on *a priori* grounds in this chapter, is practically tested in the course of the work.

CHAPTER II.

THE EXIGENCY IN EXPRESSION WHICH ABSTRACT SENTIMENT INVOLVES, AND THE STRUCTURAL PLAN OF THE GREAT MODERN INSTRUMENTAL FORMS OF COMPOSITION.

IN the last chapter I argued the natural propriety of certain general shapes of musical effect for embodying that order of moral impressure which forms the main inspiration of the poet and orator, on the grounds of the favorableness of such shapes for unfolding a powerful and elaborate rhythm; and my remarks pointed to massive and combinative musical effects, such as an *orchestra* or *chorus*, is calculated to produce: I showed that these issues of music favor the production of certain effects which the expression of abstract sentiment visibly unfolds in language. In the present chapter I shall show that there is an important exigency in expression which this order of sentiment gives rise to, and that this exigency is met in a remarkable way, in *the plan of composition* which distinguishes the higher forms of modern instrumental music as defined by great composers.

It is a peculiarity of that order of sentiment which, as it results from the higher exercise of the mind and sympathy, I term abstract to distinguish it from the instinctive type of feeling, when existing in such strength as to impel the expression of oratory, poetry, or art generally, that it does not consist of a single well defined feeling, but of a flood of various feelings—a complex moral impressure, which is ever attended by a sense of perplexity as to means of expression. With the true poetic afflatus is ever a sense that through the step-by-step character of man's powers of expression and perception, much of the thought and feeling that crowds in the breast must escape unrecorded. Thus it is that the faculty of expression consists in a great degree simply of the power of holding a crowd of ideas and feelings before the consciousness until each has been separately expressed; this is certainly the case as regards the expression of ideas and feelings in language: the greatest richness of conception may be fully represented through a moderate command of language, where there is also this muscular energy of the brain,—energy not to conceive but to hold, to grasp, that which has been conceived. The faculty of expression is thus to a great extent, the power to withhold. To make another allusion to the subject of oratory—it is to be remarked, the listener's sense of this power in the orator, constitutes a great portion of the influence he works,—the sense of matter and force withheld.

The following quotation may serve to suggest the complex nature of that moral impressure which impels art. It may be thought a morbidly forcible expression, and an exaggerated representation, of the condition in question; still, it reflects a general state of the breast which always attends contemplative habits and broad sympathy; and there is also to be taken into consideration, that in the thoughts and feelings animating the poet and musician, as in their expression, passionate energy if a fault, is a fault on the right side. It also illustrates that perplexity as to means of expression, to which I have alluded as naturally attending copiousness of conception: here the poet, either through this copiousness, or through weakness of mental grasp, feeling the difficulty of sustaining his impressions until they can be demonstrated by the halting means of language, craves for a power of spontaneous expression.

> 'Could I embody and unbosom now
> That which is most within me—could I wreak
> My thoughts upon expression, and thus throw
> Soul, heart, mind, passions, feelings, strong or weak,
> All that I would have sought, and all I seek,
> Bear, know, feel, and yet breathe—into *one* word,
> * * * * * I would speak;
> But as it is, I live and die unheard,
> With a most voiceless thought * * * *'

It is thus perceivable that the circumstances in which art is resorted to, to express abstract emotion, involve this exigency:—as there is a vast complexity of feeling to be expressed, it is necessary that the exponent possess either the faculty of holding this moral impressure before the consciousness for some length of time, or the means of throwing it into expression comparatively simultaneously. I shall attempt to show that music does supply a process of expression of the latter character; that it does this by means of a certain plan of composition which the instinct of great musicians has gradually developed, as well as through the peculiar nature of its own effect —through its *direct action* as a form of influence.

Those who are acquainted with matters relating to the history of music, are aware that instrumental music in its infancy was purely objective; that it was the musical reflection of certain well defined and broadly felt sentiments. Instrumental music was in fact, literally, 'song without words.' This objective character it still retained when it had become both elaborate and combinative in form,—when the air, tune, or theme, had become, in its instrumental repetition, fretted into variations; when the part-song had become the quartett for instruments.* In all this portion of its history instrumental music retained a character almost purely objective; it con-

* The signification of the word *objective*, as of the word *abstract*, as used in these pages, is not precise but comparative. By objective music is meant that kind of music of which the purport or object, is more distinctly defined than is the case with other kinds of music. In the same way, abstract feeling here implies feeling separated from the common contingent circumstances of emotion, and which is even of a less concrete nature than the simple feeling of life.

veyed the impression of being distinctly associated with some natural and stereotyped sentiment.

Of all old musical forms, or plans of composition, perhaps that which has influenced the musical art most deeply and permanently, is the *fugue*. It would be difficult to exaggerate the importance of the effect of this ancient form upon musical art. It is probable that the history of the fugue involves the only case of a conventional form, suggested originally by necessity, leading in a direct line to the unfolding of all the greatest subsequent treasures of an art. If dearth in the power of sustained musical expression was not itself the origin, it is certainly likely that it was a circumstance which attended the origin, of the fugue, and favored its growth. From this barrenness would ensue, in the endeavour to construct a composition of length, the necessity of repeating, imitating, or inverting, such an approach to a melody or characteristic musical idea, as could be obtained; and hence the art of elaboration would arise. If this be so, the fugue is a striking instance of restriction of the power of expression in the infancy of an art dictating a discipline of the faculties, and consummating a formula of art, without which the richest vein of inspiration destined ultimately to unfold, could not by any known means have attained its full expression. This leads me to what I have particularly to remark concerning the influence of the fugue upon music. The fugue has led to a form of musical construction which fits that important exigency in emotional expression to which I have alluded.

For the benefit of readers unacquainted with the technicalities of musical art, I will attempt to briefly explain the general form of a fugal composition.

The fugue is generally a long and elaborate composition in two, three, or four *parts*, i.e. with a dual, triple or quadruple, outline; its general peculiarity being that it represents a maximum of elaboration with a minimum of idea. Notwithstanding its length and complexity, the pure creative effort involved in the fugue, is represented by either one, two, or more short melodic passages called the *subjects* of the piece. Each *part* throughout the whole length of the composition, is composed of repetitions in various keys, of these original subjects; thus each outline, taken by itself, has little or no meaning. The general expression and meaning of the piece arises from the various juxtapositions of the *subjects*, which occur as these subjects are introduced in the *parts*.

It may be added concerning the history of this musical form, that the fugal style not only originated, but grew into full figure and power, when the vocal form of music prevailed; it is thus in the vocal department that the art itself became developed to little short of its present state. The sensible development of instrumental music follows only in the wake of the great vocal forms. Not till vocal music had become defined into the powerful and finished forms of the eighteenth century, was the fugue transplanted into the,—then modest and subordinate,—field of instrumental music, in which it has since achieved such a work of progress, where in the great principle of 'thematic treatment,' may be observed the permanent impress of its features.

In its early use, then, the fugue was, so far as it was animated by emotion at all, the expression of positive and conventional sentiment; and this character it retained throughout its most elaborate developments. At the same time in its simplest constructions may be remarked that aptitude for abstract expression from which such great results have since been developed. At that point in the construction of the simplest fugue where a counter-subject commences to follow or to interwind the original theme, is seen the origin of that plan of composition through which musical promptings of the broadest and most complex nature are now expressed. Variety in musical expression is mainly produced, not in the musically treating different sentiments, but different shades and complexions of some one sentiment. This is observable in the *aria*, which is so largely constituted by the frequent recurrence of different musical phrases applied to the same portion of the literary text, each phrase illustrating the text in an *altered sense*, as may be noticed in the songs of Handel. Now this principle of musical procedure is incorporated in the structural plan of the fugue. Where an important conception assumes the fugal form, as for instance in the case of a grand chorus, it will generally be found that the different constituent passages or subjects of the fugue, embody various phases of a single sentiment, or else different sentiments logically related. But what is to be specially noticed in this arrangement is:—the musical unfoldings of a sentiment do not inevitably occur *successively*,—do not follow one another in a perfectly free way, as in the *aria*,—but may be enunciated more or less *simultaneously*. It is through the possession of this feature by the fugue that from it has been developed a style of composition specially calculated to express abstract sentiment: for we have here a process through which a general sentiment and its various complexions may be musically enunciated comparatively simultaneously; by which, therefore, a general spontaneity conjoined to a detailed minuteness and completeness of expression, may be attained. I have observed that after sojourning in vocal music, and after having been practised into strength, the fugue became itself an instrumental form. Now in the instrumental forms belonging to the most recent development of the art the essential spirit of the fugue still obtains, in the principle of *thematic treatment*.

A composition constructed on the principle of thematic treatment, is one the main effect of which is unfolded, as in the case of the fugue, not in the production of successive musical ideas, but in the *treatment* of—the musically enlarging upon, one or two main ones. But whereas in the case of the fugue, the materials of this treatment are confined to the original subjects themselves, and the treatment itself consists of the various juxtapositions of these subjects, in the case of the composition in question, the enlarging matter may be chosen quite freely from the broad field of musical effect. The more modern form of composition is, thus, far freer than that involved in the case of the fugue,—it may, in fact, embrace all kinds of musical effect; at the same time it sufficiently resembles the fugue to combine variety with unity of character.

If we consider, then, that the mental order of sentiment ever tends to multiply and extend itself in the breast—to become an endlessly progressing train of feeling, just as the mind itself of the contemplative type, is continually moving to new impressions; that this order of sentiment thus requires a spontaneity conjoined to variety, in the process of its expression; that with regard to music, the fugue involves a process that exactly meets such a contingency; that the spirit of the fugue still regulates the structural plan of the great modern instrumental forms of music: and if we also refer to the consideration of the general aptitude of instrumental music for exemplifying rhythmic effect, —in which, as we have seen, abstract sentiment naturally tends to display itself,—we cannot fail to perceive a still further antecedent probability than was visible in the last chapter, of the modern instrumental forms proving highly favorable for becoming the vehicle for expressing the abstract order of sentiment; we cannot but be impressed with the probability that in this field of expression instrumental music unfolds its most æsthetically appropriate, as well as morally highest, function, and thus enters a range of effect which is the most powerful it can reach;—nor can we avoid thinking we can thus, to some extent, account for those prodigious expressions which in certain modern specimens of instrumental music, are consummated; and which suggest themselves as having been conceived amidst a most profound and comprehensive flow of thought and feeling.

Some considerations may be brought forward which favor the supposition that Beethoven approached instrumental composition in this spirit and employed it for this important function,—that he projected it on the basis of mental rather than instinctive, feeling; that, in fact, the revolution he worked in the spirit of instrumental music, is to be attributed to the circumstance that he was the first great genius who proceeded on this principle. With this supposition in view I shall in the following chapter, comment upon Beethoven and other great composers. In the meanwhile I have to remark that there is evidence concerning this composer's habits of work, which harmonises with the above hypothesis. It would appear that the very *modus operandi* which the poet in the lines quoted at the commencement of this chapter, felt could alone express a certain complex emotional state, is literally that which Beethoven adopted in composition,—the plan of resolving this state into a nucleus of expression—the poet's 'one word.'

In some papers on music written originally in German, and which have appeared in an English translation by Sabilla Novello, occurs the following passage. Speaking of Beethoven the author remarks:—'One of his excellencies was, he did not, like many of his predecessors and successors, force and mould into given forms, some weakly felt, ill-digested, psychological sentiment; on the contrary, he adapted the form, as far as rules of art permitted, to his own subject. When he had made himself perfectly intimate with the subject he intended to represent,—when it stood clearly and full of life before his mental vision,—a powerful brooding came over his thoughts; all the wheels of his mighty intellect were set in motion, to produce and shape the principal idea, which was to be expressed in all its different phases. He especially endeavoured to obtain the appropriate principal theme, which should announce the character of the whole piece, and impress it as clearly and decidedly as possible. He required, as a first and important condition, that it should be pregnant, like all his separate phrases.' *

It is obvious how appropriate is the habit of procedure described in the foregoing for composition in the modern instrumental forms,—how important it is, in circumstances where the greater portion of a

---

* Musikalische Briefe. Wahrheit über Tonkunst und Tonkünster. Für Freunde und Kenner. Von einem Wohlbekannten. Leipzig. 1852.
Letters about music: Truth about music and musicians for friends and connoisseurs, from one well known. Leipsic. 1852.

composition is produced by the treatment of one or two principal themes, that these themes should be pregnant in character—rich in latent expression. This habit of careful thematic selection is, in fact, the circumstance which completes the outward conditions that render this form of composition favorable for expressing abstract emotion.

It appears, then, that the difficult task of expressing a high and complex pressure of sentiment, is accomplished by music almost momentarily; that all essential expression is contained in the first outline of the tonal pencil, of which the further operations are a work of development. The question is here suggested:—how is music able to render a short theme so full of meaning; to combine so much expression with such a little material effect? The answer to this question lies to a great extent in the fact that music expresses emotion, not as all the other arts do—circuitously, by reference to some emotional incitation in outer life, or the mind; but directly, through an original medium of expression: consequently in the case of music, expression cannot be measured by effect even so nearly as poetry (unspoken), or painting can.

We may form some idea of the power music has of combining much expression with little material effect, if,—referring to language,—we consider how much meaning is sometimes suggested by the tone,—a rudimentary effect of music,—in which a single word is uttered.

The main propositions contained in this, and the preceding chapters, may be thus briefly summed up:— In ordinary speech emphasis is prompted in the expression of abstract, rather than of instinctive sentiment. Emphasis in speech, belongs to the same order of expression which in another stage of development, assumes the form of phrase in music. Massive and combinative forms of music are most favorable for exemplifying effects of phrase; and as the sole agency of musical instruments, is required for a considerable portion of the execution of such forms, the department of instrumental music may be considered their general field of display. These circumstances point to the general favorableness of abstract sentiment for forming the burthen of instrumental composition. Further;— The consideration of the nature of abstract sentiment, suggests certain conditions as necessary on the part of the demonstrator for its proper expression,—the means of effecting comprehensiveness, conjoined to spontaneity, of expression. The structural plan of the modern instrumental forms of music,—the plan of thematic treatment,—furnishes the musician with these conditions. The logical pendant to the adoption of the plan of thematic treatment, is the practice of obtaining pregnancy of theme : this is exemplified in the *modus operandi* of Beethoven.*

* It is on the same principle of the breast, which decrees more or less elaborate effects of emphasis and pause, whether in music or speech, to both express and arouse sentiment of the abstract order, that the sound of thunder or cannon, always creates an emotion of awe. How greatly the deep and measured boom of the big drum in the funeral march in 'Saul,' helps to impress the mind with the idea of Death. In that profound composition the sorrow, the regret, tell their tale in the long, sweet, mournful strains of the melody; but when at slowly recurring intervals, comes the inevitable boom of the drum,—the note of inordinate and stupendous emphasis,—the voice and feelings of the heart are momentarily hushed, but the imagination is powerfully invoked ; the sad but incidental idea of personal bereavement is suppressed, and the great, all-shadowing idea of Death, is suggested; the nature is impressed with a sense of the all-powerful, the eternal, the inevitable,— with reverence and awe. Thus, a psychological propriety could be shown to be involved by the facts, that at a funeral we toll the big bell in deep and slowly recurring *monotones ;* and on an occasion of rejoicing, make the bells peal out the full *melody* of the major scale. In the former circumstances an abstract, in the latter, a personal feeling, is involved : we mentally ponder over death, but realize joy instinctively and un- thinkingly. Again in military and national music, the higher function

of which, is to express sentiment tending to the abstract character,—sentiment inspired by such ideas as Patriotism and Heroism,—how strongly marked is the accentuation, how striking the emphasis! Remark the choral march, the 'Marseillaise!' With what a vigorous and marked accent it opens, whilst to the words of personal import the rhythm flows smoothly, and melody is conspicuous; but at the invocation, 'Aux armes!', how strongly marked again is the emphasis, and at the word 'Marchons!', how deliberately and firmly it sets in!

CHAPTER III.

A COMPARATIVE ANALYSIS OF THE SPIRIT OF THE INSTRUMENTAL MUSIC OF HAYDN, MOZART, BEETHOVEN, AND MENDELSSOHN.

A COMPARATIVE study of the instrumental works of Haydn, Mozart, Mendelssohn, and Beethoven, reveals a broad distinction separating the genius of the two former from that of the two latter composers. It may be said that Haydn and Mozart are musicians by instinct, whilst Mendelssohn and Beethoven are musicians by thought. The sweet, rich strains flowing so copiously from the two former composers, may be likened to the beauty of an infant, which effuses unattended by effort, and in the utmost simplicity. In this music we see two simple and almost childlike natures the receptacle of the grandest endowments, and the agency of a most sublime function; yet the inspiration comes almost unsought—

is unfolded in ease and complacency, and the characters over which it passes, preserve throughout their normal simplicity.

On the other hand, in the production of the music of Beethoven and Mendelssohn, the individual character is not at all a passive, quiescent thing in the matter; it is active and obtrusive throughout. The strains of these masters do not *come*, as the numbers came to Pope, or as the music of Haydn and Mozart came to them; but they are intellectually wrested from nature, and have the strong impress of character upon them.

The music of Haydn and Mozart is not inconsistent with what we should imagine might proceed from natures amiable, submissive to circumstances that be, with full content, happy, cheerful and taking pleasure in all things. The natures of Beethoven and Mendelssohn as betrayed in their works, though differing widely, unite in forming in one respect, a strong contrast to this picture, for there is in both the opposite of content; there is restlessness, aspiration— a yearning for fuller and higher existence. Both of these masters forsake the joys of the quiescent mind and passive nature, and search, though in different directions, for others. Notwithstanding a keen desire to avoid entering the regions of fancy, I am tempted to continue,—that Beethoven's world of aspiration seems redolent of nature—nature purified and divested of death,—a 'new earth;' whilst Mendelssohn's, is at one time 'some delicious land' of poetic imagining, at another, the spiritual world of religion. With Haydn and Mozart our inward nature is elevated but not in any abnormal way. With Mendelssohn and Beethoven our spirit is invoked from us and led a far and mystic chase : this music reflects a sympathy in its conceivers, for an immortal state, a craving for an ineffable beauty—for a great consolation.

The relative extent to which the music of these four masters bears comment, must not be taken as the measure of its respective merit. That music which most suggests remark, may be neither better nor even more original, than that about which we cannot find a word to say. The musical organization in Haydn and Mozart, was so ripe and perfect as to effuse music without the excitement of conditions beyond the musical instinct itself,—such as the original moral idiosyncrasy of Beethoven, and the highly cultivated mind of Mendelssohn.

There may exist in the breast a certain emotional afflatus which arises spontaneously. It is not positive emotion, created by any particular outward influence; it is more a general and broad *desire to feel* than actual and definite feeling. As physical power exists latently stored up in the frame before it is manifested in outward movement, and when thus existing in great force, creates a vague and strong desire for action quite irrespectively of external incentive; so intellectual power exists latently in the inward nature, and when in strong force, imbues a like vague but intense desire to vent itself in some form of demonstration. To such primordial force as this all art-creation is owing. In its exudation it may involve instinctive, or abstract emotion; and become demonstrated in music, poetry, painting, or literature according to other circumstances attending the nature of the individual. If the mental faculties,—reason, imagination, —are largely developed, they will tend to induce this moral energy to the regions of contemplation, and it will probably resolve itself into definite emotion of the abstract order; but if this is not the case, it will be more likely to operate in adding strength and intensity to the instinctive feelings. In the same way it is highly probable that the demonstration of this moral afflatus, whatever emotion it may resolve itself into, depends upon what particular demonstrative faculties preponderate in the nature. If, for instance, those outer faculties which relate to sound,—a keen discrimination and appreciation of tonal effects, and the faculty of devising such effects,—exist in a high state of development, and they are the most perfect faculties of the higher physical nature, it is likely that it will be demonstrated by *music;* but if those faculties which relate to visual effect,—form, colour, &c.,—are developed in this degree and proportion, then it will probably become manifested through the art of *painting.* Thus, if this be true, upon the condition of the faculties of the moral nature, depends the type of emotion which original moral energy assumes; and upon the condition of the faculties of the higher physical nature, depends the form of manifestation— the art, in which that emotion becomes demonstrated.

Now in the case of all the arts save music, it is

essential before art-effect is consummated, that the original energy be directed to some distinct object, so as to involve a definite phase of feeling,—it is so because all art manifestation except that of music, takes place through natural images, feeling being expressed by the reproduction of its incentive in outward nature. But music on the other hand, so far as the material or form of expression is concerned, is, in the expression of emotion, quite independent; it cannot copy external phenomena, but by its remarkable powers of pure expression, imparts sentiment in a direct manner. As, then, the reproduction of the outward incentive to feeling, is not essential to musical expression, we see no obstacle to that original moral energy which has been mentioned as preceding all art, inspiring music without having become previously resolved into distinct feelings; such an art expression as this would be fraught with feeling, though of an indefinite kind, and might be tinged with the complexion of various emotions according to the thoughts, fancies, and feelings existing at the time in the breast of the composer; its meaning might be beautiful and deep, though veiled, and it would impress strongly those who heard it because its animating soul is that moral force out of which all emotion is born.

It is not improbable that the freer and more unpremeditated part of the great portion of instrumental works, more particularly those of Haydn and Mozart, was composed under these circumstances. It may also be generally stated that the moral energy of these composers tends towards instinctive emotion, whereas in the case of Beethoven and Mendelssohn,—they being more frequently drawn by the power of their minds, into the realms of thought and meditation,—such energy tends to abstract emotion.

Regarding the music of Beethoven and Mendelssohn on the one hand, and that of Haydn and Mozart on the other, we see, also, in the one case strikingly exemplified the advantages and disadvantages to musical expression, when into its inspiration enters more or less the influence of the mind; and in the other, the unique, ripe, and generally less assumptive character that it bears, when springing from the unprompted action of the musical instinct. In the case of the former two composers there is mental,—it may be poetical or philosophical,—*pressure* brought to bear upon the conception of emotion and musical idea. The chief advantage of an active reflective faculty attending the musical instinct is, that it will be likely to invoke the voice of music to the utterance of a more elevated order of emotion; the music will accordingly be more poetical, thoughtful, and uniformly dignified. But of those who are gifted with the wings of poetry and meditation, few can carry into their flight the full strength of the sympathy, so as to *feel strongly* the emotions which the mind calls into being.* In the case of Mendelssohn's instrumental music, for instance, there is a certain industrious fancy involved rather than true imagination, consequently the sympathy is

* This faculty of carrying the full force of the sympathy into the workings of the imagination, is the source of all living power and vivid truthfulness in creative art. As graphic power in literary description, is little more than the transcript of a perfect and clear inward realization of the scenes and circumstances described, so dramatic power proceeds from the strong realization in the dramatist, of the circumstances *imagined*, and thus of the feelings suggested. In the case of the novelist, the well drawn character, is the character that is first well *realised* in the writer's imagination. With regard to the painter also, the more vividly he realises his conception of a desired effect, the more real and forcible will its representation appear. What is seen distinctly will always be pourtrayed clearly, and what is felt deeply will always be expressed forcibly; and this applies to that which may be seen and felt in the imagination.

but weakly aroused; the feelings called to action by the mind, thus being but feebly and briefly realised, the musical faculty is not strongly invoked or deeply inspired. Music thus produced, has not the perspicuity and natural beauty of music spontaneously inspired, neither does it possess the deep expression and marked feature of music arising in an earnest flow of the abstract order of feeling. Thus it is, that while the music of Mendelssohn is bold, original, graceful, and beautiful in its physical form, its spirit is frequently shadowy, airy, and unreal. Being the offspring of fancy rather than of deep imagination, its sentiment is weakly felt and therefore weakly impressed, and its really fine tonal effect appears to wear an artificial expression.* Beethoven on the other hand, is one of

* The reader will observe that in these remarks I abstain from comparisons relating to the material construction and development of the art of Music. I criticise the spirit not the form, of the works to which allusion is made; and pass over the relative technical merits and peculiarities of the composers. If the above mentioned composers were compared solely with reference to the purely musical merits of their works—to the power and skill to wield the implement of tonal effect, which these works betray, and not with reference to the moral element contained, then the names of Mendelssohn and Mozart, would occupy a more marked position in this general comparison. For instance, in the power of conducting his subjects through every variety of musical involution with the happiest skill and taste, Mozart appears superior to

the few instances of a nature that can carry true warmth and strength of feeling,—in fact, the full force of the sympathy,--into his imaginative conceptions. The emotion which his mind called to action was thus strongly felt, and the music inspired is correspondingly earnest in character and forcible in expression.

There is, however, a character in Beethoven's music, which seems to be less the result of a naturally active mind than of a mind spurred to action by certain exceptional conditions attending it. There is observable in many of his calm, melodic movements, with the fulness of expression and sensuous beauty suggestive of Mozart and Haydn, the mingling of a deep and mournful aspiration; and in many of his energetic movements, a convulsive character suggestive

Beethoven. But the two masters brought to the task of composition a widely different spirit of action. The skill with which Mozart could develop any subject,—the power he possessed of weaving into a wonderful tonal fabric, any thread of melody,—may have rendered him careless in the selection of his subjects for composition; having adopted one, he carries it through an endless series of changes, seldom relinquishing it until every mode of treatment that it will bear, has been exhausted. Beethoven on the other hand, selects his subject as containing a certain latent moral burden, and when he has so developed it as to fully unfold its inner spirit, he relinquishes it.

of a purturbed mind. This last moral circumstance, indeed, overshadowed largely the composition of Beethoven's later works.

There are considerations which go to show that mental depression is calculated to operate generally in a way highly disadvantageous to musical composition. It is not the first impulse of the breast possessed with the actual feeling of grief, to turn to art for expression and solace. Consistently with the traditional relation between knowledge and woe only in reversed position, the tendency of the latter in man, is not to incite art, but pure mental action—to stir the mind to search out the cause and moral propriety of its suffering, and thus to discover consolation or reconciliation. There is an intuitive tendency in the breast under the smart of misfortune, more especially when this is of a moral nature, to seek out some general principle of which the particular grief that may be in question, is an exemplification. Disappointed minds have a strong tendency to generalise. This is the endeavour of the nature to merge its misfortunes in the action of some high, unswerving law; this accomplished, the heart bows down before an influence alike inevitable and imposing, the imagination is kindled, the moral existence expands, and the spirit rises. Where the intellect is not profound enough to connect a petty grief with some grand principle in the dispensation of life, then this moral instinct of self protection, impels the mind to discover, if not the first cause of its sorrow, in the grand field of philosophy and morality, at least some likeness of it in the beauty and sublimity of nature; hence many a striking *simile*. This is the process through which the nature of man morally surmounts its afflictions. It is a process of reconciliation. Through it, the lost hope and broken sympathy, from being unnoticeable fragments of ruin strewing the moral highway of life, become the testimony of some great law in the government of the world. This is the history of much profound and solemn philosophy.

Thus it is that literature, as it affords fullest scope for the record and expression of pure mental exercise, accords better than art with sorrowful minds. But music, notwithstanding its aptitude for being tinctured with melancholy, is the natural resort of a buoyant spirit. As I have suggested, personal depression may certainly develop habits of thought and meditation; and it is true that these habits in a composer, tend to elevate considerably the character of his music: thus depression may, in certain circumstances by reason of its effect on the mind, have a favorable influence on musical inspiration; but its general effect is highly unfavorable to this inspiration. The general art-impulse proceeds from fulness of joy. The definite emotion common to the birth of all art, is the emotion of admiration: art rises in a desire to express and communicate an over full and fine sense of this emotion. Moreover, in the case of music and painting, this expression is consummated by the elevated exercise of the higher physical senses. Now as the pleasure naturally produced by the action of these senses, is great in the degree that that action is fine and elevated, it is obvious that these arts to reflect emotion faithfully, must be exercised in a spirit of great joy,—I mean a spirit of joy in a wide sense—in a sense capable of embracing the most elevated moral condition of the breast.

It is thus perceivable why depression is a generally unfavorable concomitant of musical composition. In admitting the possibility of its having at times a beneficial influence on composition through creating habits of reflection, this fact should be taken into consideration:—thought may involve the highest mental exercise and deepest mental interest, and yet far from gratify the sympathy. From the foregoing considerations it is obvious, such thought must involve an emotional condition the opposite of favorable for musical inspiration. On the other hand, thought which warms and expands the sympathy, is the most favorable circumstance that can attend the exercise of the musical faculty.

We here see how the element of personal depression in Beethoven's moral condition, must have interfered with the natural action of the musical faculty,— which ought to be the voice of rapture in some form or other; we may also see the possibility of the continual opening up of the sombre channels of reflection, in a mind not needing any incentive to activity, operating in a way unfavorable for music. We are also here in a position to understand why the absence of all exceptional features from the instrumental strains of Haydn and Mozart, is in some respects a gain rather than a loss to the music. As in the case of these composers, the art-impulse was not stimulated so specially as in the case of Beethoven and Mendelssohn, but arose in a more spontaneous manner out of the general moral energy of the breast, the musical faculty was in no danger of being pushed to inordinate and strained action—to catch effects beyond its grasp. In the slow movements of Haydn, there breathes solemnity, grandeur, beauty, and all that is most elevated in expression, but there is no longing. All is suffused in an atmosphere of content, and however deeply solemn the strains may be, the voice of a sigh is not heard. It would thus appear that the music of Haydn and Mozart is of a kind particularly perfect as music. Throughout the course it takes into the depths of expression there are betrayed no evidences of disparity between conception and realization.

I have referred to the hypothesis that the great abstract-instrumental style of composition was first decidedly exemplified by Beethoven. Some features of his system of proceeding in composition, have been described. He first resolved his musical promptings into a nucleus of expression. He took special pains to inwardly weigh that succession of notes which was to form his main subject. Its characteristic must be that of pregnancy—of containing in embryo the spirit of the subsequent expression. This system of proceeding, was certainly, to a great extent, the cause of the distinctive character of Beethoven's music. The subjects of nearly all composers but him, are short melodies of the ordinary character, emanating from emotion of the instinctive type; or else a short series of notes arranged with no other object than the production of a pointed effect so contrived as to admit of the various treatments of musical science. A subject of the former kind being the expression of some natural feeling, would be far more effective if instead of being played, it was sung with words containing a narrative of such circumstances as might naturally attend that feeling. On the principle of making this kind of subject the basis of an instrumental work, the germ of a work of this kind might be extracted from an Opera-song. And notwithstanding this has been done with great effect in the case of Operatic overtures, it is questionable whether such a method of procedure is calculated to lead generally to good art.*

In the first place the composer is in danger of becoming spasmodic, who proceeds to base an instrumental work upon a subject belonging to that class of melodies which derive their general expression from emotion of the instinctive order; a vigorous treatment of a subject of this kind, is likely to produce effects which sound vaguely earnest and unmeaningly passionate. With respect to art generally, it is obvious that forcible manifestations of instinctive feeling, are only consistently the subject of art when their cause is shown; if a literary passage containing one, and belonging to one of the characters in a drama, was declaimed apart from the rest of the drama, it is unnecessary to say that

* This form of composition has claims to æsthetic legitimacy even when not conceived and framed in accordance with the principle of abstract instrumental composition. As both abstract and instinctive emotion are the subject of musical expression in the Opera, they may appropriately be so in its overture. When the main features of the latter consist of passages extracted bodily from the former, the overture may be regarded as a brief preliminary summary of the Opera itself, not as an abstract work inspired by the general spirit of the Opera, which in these circumstances, would form the subject of moral contemplation. Overture and Opera being considered one work, the latter reveals the circumstances to which the sentimental melodies of the former refer, and thus renders them a consistent portion of Instrumental music.

the effect however forcible, would be meaningless.* And if it is not so absurd for a strain illustrating some passionate outburst or fervent expression, of instinctive feeling, to be musically enunciated in a symphony, as for this emotion to be verbally declaimed unattended by those circumstances to which it relates, it is still naturally incongruous.

In the second place, material disadvantages are incurred by using a subject of this character as a germ from which to unfold a series of instrumental effects. Instrumental composition should of course involve a musical form calculated for embracing those effects which an instrument or orchestra can best produce, such as antiphonal, concerted, and bold rhythmic effects; but it has been shown that these are naturally connected with the expression of the abstract order of sentiment. Again, as an instinctive feeling is elicited not by the objects revealed by

* It is equally obvious that if an important *soliloquy* in the piece, was thus declaimed, the effect would be perfectly consistent because it would be the expression of feeling which naturally arose solitarily. The fact that an expression of instinctive feeling is only made under special outward circumstances, and that an expression of abstract sentiment may be made under *any* outward circumstances, has, thus, some bearing upon musical art.

thought but by the palpable objects of life, it is, though compact and forcible, finite and unexpansive, —it does not give rise to new feelings—to a progressive train of emotions. A closely faithful art-expression of such a feeling as this, will thus naturally be comparatively indiffusive,—it will not tend to give rise to copiousness of effect; it must thus be an unsatisfactory basis for long compositions, of a varied yet homogeneous character, and possessing a sustained poetical weight,—yet this is a part of the essential character of an effective instrumental work.

Beethoven's subjects certainly give the impression that they are the emanation of abstract sentiment. As the sweet, tender strains of songs and dances, are felt to be the expression of the emotions of love, joy, sorrow, or hope; so the at one time grand, at another, simple, but always portentous series of notes forming Beethoven's subject, is felt as the expression of the feeling which arises solitarily, being born of thought, and having for its object nothing the influence of which depends only upon personal association, but things of both intrinsic beauty and broad suggestiveness, such as moral charms, nature's forms and actions, her power and grandeur. Further support may be brought to the hypothesis that he composed his instrumental works in this spirit. A distinguishing feature of his genius, is the production of pieces which though they are in one place exuberantly gay, in another, deeply serious, do not express either personal depression or cheerfulness. In the greater portion of his music, excepting perhaps the very short movements, and the slow movements, there is geniality in earnestness, and depth in gaiety: the music thus elevates as it moves, and impresses as it gladdens. This quality in the music, harmonises with the idea that it expresses emotion involved between its author and outward nature, rather than that arising from personal relations or incidental circumstances. How the sense of cheerfulness and seriousness produced by the music, resembles our impression of those feelings when produced by nature! Nature in her gayest aspects, never imbues a cheerfulness devoid of seriousness,—never fails to impress as well as please; and in her grand and solemn phases, whilst she imbues seriousness, she does not sadden but strengthens and elevates. These aspects of nature are ever homogeneous; and the different phases of feeling they imbue, pass through the breast without producing discordant changes. The passages of various character in the music in question, are also homogeneous; and where one markedly gay is immediately succeeded by another strikingly serious, no moral inconsistency is felt. With respect to these qualities, this music appears to breathe no egotism; its gaiety and seriousness do not seem reflective of the fluctuation of narrow interests and minor circumstances. It seems rather the expression of the mind absorbed in nature, personal self-consciousness being suppressed, the cheerfulness and seriousness it breathes, as is the case with these qualities when nature imbues them, including one-another.

When a composer commences an instrumental work with a subject inspired by this order of sentiment, how appropriate and effective, for the work of development, are the orchestra's resources for exemplifying bold rhythmic design, and producing combinative and antiphonal effects! As abstract emotion involves a progressive train of feelings, and thus tends to fill the nature more and more largely with a sense of all that is elevated and morally impressive, a strain of music born of this order of feeling, must be favorable to extensive enlargement, and well fitted for the purpose of unfolding the more powerful order of musical effects without sacrificing poetic unity or natural congruity.

With a view to still further elucidate that division in spirit which I have hitherto referred to as visible in music only, I append some quotations having reference to the art of painting, in the spirit of which, as it appears, a similar division is also observable.*

'You will find it a pregnant question, if you follow it forth, and leading to many others, not trivial, Why it is, that in Sir Joshua's girl, or Gainsborough's, we always think first of the Ladyhood; but in Giotto's, of the Womanhood? Why, in Sir Joshua's hero, or Vandyck's, it is always the Prince or the Sir, whom we see first; but in Titian's, the man.'

* The principle on which I have made a division in the spirit of music, coincides so nearly with that on which a division in the spirit of painting, is implied in these quotations as to render the supposition reasonable in the absence of circumstantial knowledge, that my tone of comment was suggested by them: this was not the case. My text was written to beyond this point, before the writings from which I quote, appeared.

'Not that Titian's gentlemen are less finished than Sir Joshua's; but their gentlemanliness is not the principal thing about them; their manhood absorbs, conquers, wears it as a despised thing. Nor—and this is another stern ground of separation—will Titian make a gentleman of every one he paints. He will make him so if he is so, not otherwise; and this not only in general servitude to truth, but because in his sympathy with deeper humanity, the courtier is not more interesting to him than any one else. "You have learned to dance and fence; you can speak with clearness, and think with precision; your hands are small, your senses acute, and your features well shaped. Yes; I see all this in you, and will do it justice. You shall stand as none but a well-bred man could stand; and your fingers shall fall on the sword-hilt as no fingers could but those that knew the grasp of it. But for the rest, this grisly fisherman, with rusty cheek and rope-frayed hand, is a man as well as you. * * His bronze colour is quite as interesting to me, Titian, as your paleness, and his hoary spray of stormy hair takes the light as well as your waving curls. Him also will I paint, with such picturesqueness as he may have; yet not putting the picturesqueness first in him, as in you I have not put the gentlemanliness first. In him I see a strong human creature, contending with all hardship; in you also a human creature, uncontending, and possibly not strong. Contention or strength, weakness or picturesqueness, and all other such accidents in either, shall have due place. But the immortality and miracle of you—this clay that burns, this colour that changes—are in truth the awful things in both; these shall be first painted—and last." ' *

The following quotation shows that objects of the most conventional character, may be represented in the high abstract frame of mind—in such a way that those qualities calculated to appeal to the higher sympathy, are prominent. 'In the portrait of the Hausmann George Gyzen, every accessory is perfect with a fine perfection; the carnations in the glass vase by his side—the ball of gold, chased with blue enamel, suspended on the wall—the books—the steel yard—the papers on the table—the seal ring, with its quartered bearings,—all intensely there, and there in beauty of which no

* 'Reynolds and Holbein.' *Cornhill Magazine*, 1862.

one could have dreamed that even flowers or gold were capable, far less parchment or steel. But every change of shade is felt, every rich and rubied line of petal followed; every subdued gleam in the soft blue of the enamel, and bending of the gold, touched with a hand whose patience of regard creates rather than paints. The jewel itself was not so precious as the rays of enduring light which form it, and flash from it, beneath that errorless hand.' *

By aid of the following quotation, I am enabled to broaden my statement of the two main tones of feeling,—the instinctive, and the abstract. 'Solitude of soul, and introspection, and the melancholy which loves to be alone with nature, have a place in modern pyschology. A morbid sense of isolation results, which has been admirably depicted by Goethe in his Faust. This character, to classic thinkers, would have seemed unreal and monstrous in the last degree. They would have shrunk from its unhealthy self-analysis and constant brooding over private pains. But in modern society it has a deep and far-spread truth. It represents a condition of human life which is almost universal,

* 'Reynolds and Holbein.' *Cornhill Magazine*, 1862.

and which constitutes the special gravity of modern, as distinct from ancient modes of thought. The vast importance of the individual in the face of nature and of God is here asserted. Faust, in the anguish of his scepticism, looking at the moonlight, longs to be far off upon the hills, or on the meadows, and to bathe his pain away in mingled light and dew. When passion is struggling with the sense of duty in his soul, he seeks the mountains. We find him among trees and caverns, listening to the tempest and endeavouring to lose his human troubles in the contemplation of eternal nature. Again, after the catastrophe of Margaret's episode it is among the fields, and pines, and waterfalls of Switzerland that Faust recruits his shattered strength.

'Nature is always made the antidote of human ills. Its peace contrasts with our unrest, its broken continuity with our changefulness, the order of its recurring seasons with our chaotic history, the durability of its powers with our ephemeral lease of life, its calm indifference with our fretfulness and intolerance of pain. Shakspeare, in his play of *As You Like It*, has expressed this aspect of modern sentiment with regard to nature. The lyrics 'Under the greenwood tree,' and 'Blow, blow, thou winter wind,' most delicately point the contrast we have tried to draw. But since the days of Shakspeare the love of natural beauty has increased and been developed. He, and the men of his time, cared for the colours, and the scents, and the freshness of the outer world with the keen sensibilities of youth. Man was still uppermost in their thoughts. They loved the earth as a pleasure-ground in which he passed his time. The idea of nature as a vast power—instinct with divinity, from which the human soul, in solitude, might draw great thoughts and inspirations—had not yet occurred to them. They did not find in landscape a mirror of their own emotions, or transfer the feelings of humanity to inanimate objects.

'This kind of pantheistic reverence has grown up of late years. Rousseau led to it by the doctrine which he preached of returning to a state of nature. In the old age of feudal civilization men imagined a golden period of youth, before the growth of statecraft and class prerogatives. Naked savage life appeared to them, half throttled by the chains and bandages of centuries, to be the true condition of the human race. And when the throes which shook Europe, destroying the old forms of social order, had produced a scepticism in the hearts of many, Nature and her undisturbed repose became the only refuge for them in the tumult of the world. Removing their faith from man, and from the god of his imagination, they reposed it in Nature, and in the spirit that controlled the elements. In England, Wordsworth became the high-priest of this creed. Shelley, and Keats, and Coleridge, each in his own way, contributed to render it permanent and influential over thought. The point in which they all agreed, was reverence for Nature as the source of intellectual enjoyment and moral instruction. They were not content with the slight attention which had been paid to her more superficial aspects by preceding poets. They ransacked her deeper secrets, dwelling alone with her, exercising their powers of observation on the minutest incidents, and making pictures from hitherto neglected scenes. Man, in truth, had descended from the high tower of his humanity, whence he had been wont to cast a careless and half-patronizing eye upon the hills and pastures that surrounded him. From that time forward he has learned to recognize that not only are men interesting to mankind, but that also in the world itself there is a dignity and loveliness which he must study with humility and patience. This is a great lesson, the whole value of which has hardly yet been recognized. But the progress of the age in physical science, and in the facilities of locomotion, tend to make it every day more widely felt. The more we know of the universe, as revealed to us by chemistry, geology, astronomy, and all our other instruments of discovery, the less we boast that man is the centre of all things. The world and its immensity necessarily occupy our thoughts more duly than in days when wars and politics and metaphysical discussion filled the minds of men. And while we traverse new countries to satisfy our curiosity, or for the sake of health and pleasure, the various objects of natural interest presented to our eyes, explained by science, or admired for their intrinsic beauty, must extend our observation, and distract our cares from petty griefs and from the sense of personal importance.'[*]

[*] *Position of Landscape Painting in England.* Cornhill Magazine, 1865.

To compose in the abstract-instrumental style requires more than absolute genius and skill. The true abstract composer must be imbued with the high poetic temper. Thought as well as feeling must animate him. As well as delighting in sweet sounds, appreciating the ordinary influences of beauty, and being susceptible of the instinctive sentiments, he must be sensitive to moral beauty, feel that sublimity met in the higher walks of contemplation, sympathise with the great in nature and the human soul,—in short, be filled with homage for all beauty, and with aspiration to all worthiness.

CHAPTER IV.

THE INTELLECTUAL POSITION OF INSTRUMENTAL MUSIC.

IN the course of this work, I have frequently alluded to an order of feeling which is natural to man, yet very different from what is understood by natural feeling; to emotion of which the channels do not lie exclusively between man and man, but between man and nature generally: and I have endeavoured to show not only that instrumental music is specially fitted to form the expression of this feeling,[*] but that it is unfitted for the expression of instinctive feeling, the grounds of this latter proposition being :—(1) As instinctive feeling involves special personal circumstances, it is incongruous when exhibited divested of them. (2) It does not naturally impel forcible or elaborate effects of accent, yet these are a portion of

[*] See page 41.

the effects which an instrument or an orchestra can best produce. (3) As it is of a compact, unexpansive, and finite character, a *subject* that is animated by it, is not well fitted to be the text, or germ, of a long composition of varied, and yet homogeneous character, which are the necessary qualities of an effective instrumental work.

The suitableness in the above circumstances of a subject inspired by abstract feeling, which results from the expansive nature of this feeling, has also been added to the list of those considerations which show that for its expression instrumental music has special powers.

It may be asked:—Of what use are these considerations,—are they calculated to practically influence the art of music? That to some extent they are calculated to do this through only the fact of their being drawn from the observation of life, will appear in the next chapter; in the meantime it may be remarked, that they undoubtedly furnish us with some criterion, though a very insufficient one, whose application extends beyond the form and technicalities of the art, a criterion namely, of its spirit, which has long been a desideratum. In order to rank with poetry and painting as a truly elevating art and belonging to those lasting influences which aid man to progress, music should possess general as well as only material symmetry. Yet hitherto the moral source and intention of instrumental music, have not been even definitely indicated : it has been felt that obscurity in these respects, does not set well upon a branch of art for which a high dignity is claimed; consequently, there has been much groping,—many explanations more or less plausible, having been made, mingled with frivolous accounts of what authors intended their works to express. On the basis of the considerations thus far laid down, I submit that the expression of at least a grand type of emotion, may with some reasonableness, be pointed at, as the function of grand instrumental music; that music like poetry and painting, has its high abstract walk; that, like these, she is not always the voice of instinct, or the beguiler of sense, but may be at times moved by the currents of man's higher nature, and form a portion of the record of that which is essentially high and immortal in him. And if I have only been able to point to a type of emotion as the inspiration and burden of grand instrumental music—to describe these with generalities, I may point to the fact that little more than this can be done in the case of any art. In great pictures, the objects, —that is to say, all those features that strike the eye and the mind most distinctly,—constitute only the frame-work of their meaning. In such works, varieties of form and colour, corresponding with sound and accent in music, are only the material channels of the high purport of the work; and though the former are the likeness of natural things, the reproduction of them is not the painter's ultimate object. The higher purport of a picture is couched in its expressiveness, —which is lofty, in the degree that it is spiritual,*— and this is, taken as a whole, little less undefinable than that of great instrumental compositions. In the case of a picture, certain portions of the expressiveness, are seen to relate directly to certain definitely

* The utmost glory of the human body is a mean subject of contemplation, compared to the emotion, exertion, and character of that which animates it; the lustre of the limbs of the Aphrodite is faint beside that of the brow of the Madonna; and the divine form of the Greek god, except as it is the incarnation and expression of divine mind, is degraded beside the passion and the prophecy of the vaults of the Sistine.— *Modern Painters, by John Ruskin.*

revealed circumstances; but can all the expressiveness be thus explained? and is not the vague suggestiveness of such a work—its power of creating high, illimitable, and undefined feeling,—such as that sense of mystery and immortality, which the writer of a passage quoted in the last chapter, imagines Titian as having felt upon beholding the 'clay that burns,' the 'colour that changes,'—its really sublime attribute? The high phases of every art suggest great, comprehensive truth; they all point more or less directly to the mystic source of that which is glorious in outward nature, and heroic within: whatever may be their subject, they work one influence upon the breast—imbue the sense of a beauty that is ineffable, a virtue that is all potent; and open up feeling which may vary as to intensity in different breasts, yet in each, will be of one broad nature, and fall into the same grand channels of awe and homage. Pencil, pen, and lyre alike strive to express the sympathy of the human soul, with all that is great in deed and grand in aspect,—a sympathy as infinite as its inspiration, and whose tale of expression is never ended.

Thus the full meaning of the higher efforts of the

painter, can be probed little more closely than in the case of co-ordinate works of musical art. The fact of the materials of the painter's art expression, being the likeness of natural things, may lead a shallow observer to suppose that in this likeness exists the whole purport of the work. And because the materials of musical expression, are not the exact likeness of anything in nature or life, instrumental music through like imperfect observation, has been assumed to have no meaning. In having then indicated a certain great type of emotion, as the inspiration and spirit of grand instrumental music; in having suggested that from this type of feeling the moral element animating the higher phases of all art, is drawn; and in having shown that the quality of indefinitude belongs to the higher portion of the expressiveness of all works of art, and thus of itself, does not evince meagreness of moral purport, I believe that I have shown that this species of music occupies a moral plane in common with the great works of fine art generally. The fact alone of an art being a recognized instrument of moral exposition, has an important practical influence on that art. Without this recognition, no art is held in high and permanent honour; and it need scarcely be said, that although the absence of human esteem, does not in every instance prevent the production of great works, it leaves a cold atmosphere for art-growth. On the other hand, if a certain high order of feeling is associated with a certain path of art, the result is, to draw to that art this very order of feeling,—as the fact of cathedral architecture and religious paintings having been a recognized expression of religious feeling, drew to the execution of such works, a spirit which greatly conduced to develop the grandeur, beauty, and purity that many of them breathe. These facts :— that this art had a definite moral standing ground; that it was held in highest honour, and was regarded as a most momentous branch of endeavour, favoured the growth of a spirit appropriate for animating it, by imbuing those who approached it, with a sense of seriousness and of emulation, and by insuring that no art-impulse worthy to invest it, should fail to be drawn to it. In the same way, the composer will be more likely to bring a uniformly high and dignified vein of thought and feeling, to the task of instrumental composition, when it is generally acknowledged as the expression of the same order of sentiment as that which invests the sister arts in their loftiest phases, than he is at present likely to do, there being now no fixed respect surrounding it, and no moral function distinctly associated with it; in attempting this style of music, he will then, at least sweep all frivolous and commonplace garniture from the chambers of the mind, and clear them for higher vesture.

These considerations may prove indirectly beneficial to music, if they suggest the desirableness of composers looking at times to a higher and more varied source of inspiration than the hackneyed incitation of the instinctive feelings; if they point to the emancipation of the musical mind, from a too narrow round of associations—remind it that other than technical knowledge should possess it—that the source of music is not music but the general mental and moral stream, and impress it with the necessity of habits of reflection. For the musician, amidst those whose road is a special and deeply sunk groove, is peculiarly liable to lose the habit of broad mental activity, partly because he has to spend much time in mechanical practice and technical study, and partly through the fact that musical art-material, by reason of its intrinsic beauty, may be made to assume a pleasing form when only animated by the slightest moral impulse.

The true destiny of the musical, as of the whole art mind, is to walk in those high paths of knowledge attained by the advanced mind of man, and to survey the full intellectual scene around. The want of this salutary mental activity, is the cause of that monotony which now characterises the musical cast of expression notwithstanding the variety that was imported into it during the period occupied by Haydn, Mozart, Beethoven, and Mendelssohn. Some of this monotony is caused by the frequency with which musical phrases fall into the same hackneyed idioms, and express the same emotional phases ; and the desire to break through it, forms doubtless not a small portion of that impulse which has given rise to the new German school. By whatever means the desired change is eventually wrought, it will be greatly stimulated by enlarged culture and the broad spirit of modern thought, becoming established in the musical mind.

CHAPTER V.

THE PRINCIPLES ON WHICH THE MUSICAL AND LITERARY PLAN OF AN OPERA, SHOULD BE BASED.

IN dramatic composition the musician has to deal with personal and abstract feeling intermingled. In an important drama, as well as those minor circumstances which occasion the display of natural feeling, there are generally some broad principles in agitation, such as religion, liberty, &c., and some occurrences on a grand scale, which spur the mind to action, excite the imagination, and thus arouse abstract emotion. He also here meets the circumstance of natural feeling approaching abstract, in the qualities of grandeur and sublimity: a wife, husband, sister, brother, or friend, may be represented as displaying loftiness of soul and heroism of act. Yet the moral element thus unfolded, is still distinct from abstract sentiment, being without its breadth, impersonal nature, and permanent vitality; it is instinctive feeling in its loftiest manifestation. How different, for instance, as regards breadth and permanency of, character, are the following two classes of feelings :— on the one hand, faithful love, and friendship, in their keenest manifestation; on the other, patriotism, loyalty, constancy to religious tenets, love of freedom, the passion for nature—art—knowledge, &c. Whereas the incentive of the former feelings, is a personal one, and the feelings tend to assert the personality of their possessor, the incentive of the latter, is something permanent and comprehensive, and the feelings tend to suppress the personality of whom they invest. Whereas also the former feelings, after arriving at a season of vivid life, tend to subside and to dwell calmly in the breast, the latter, are remarkable for their permanently passionate hold upon the nature.

From what has been said concerning the specialities of intonation and accentuation it follows that those musical forms which involve bold and broad rhythmic outline,—the choral and orchestral forms,—are best fitted for illustrating the broad ideas—for expressing the abstract emotion, in a drama; and that the more keenly expressive—the more melodic forms, are best fitted for expressing the personal sentiment. I do not, of course, state this fact with the idea that a mechanical rule for composition, can be formed either from it, or in any other way; but as a general principle which the composer to a great extent intuitively exemplifies, and a knowledge of which may prove both interesting, and, as I shall hereafter endeavour to show, advantageous to him. It may, however, be thought that this principle cannot apply strictly to dramatic music; it is not, for instance, an unfrequent thing in a drama, for emotions belonging to both the main orders of feeling, to unfold almost, if not quite simultaneously: this condition of things, according to the principle laid down, demands a musical effect into which both bold emphasis and soft melody, enter and intermingle. Now, as in a piece of music, each *part* is an essential portion of the structure, it may be asked:—can one piece of music express sentiment of these two orders? I answer that one piece of music can do this; that various feelings may be felt simultaneously, and that music, through that power of condense expression it possesses by reason of the impalpable nature of its effect, and with the more mechanical aid of its feature, harmony, and the power it has of producing effects of now graduated loudness, now successive loudness and softness, now simultaneous loudness and softness, —a power which may be compared to *perspective* in painting,—can express emotion in a complex as well as in a simple condition. If, however, this principle is couched in the natural laws of human demonstration, we may expect to see it to some extent already exemplified. As a case in point, may be mentioned Mozart's, *Il mio tesoro*, which is generally acknowledged to be one of the finest dramatic airs in existence. In this air, where personal sentiment is expressed soft melody is all in all to the effect, and the single human voice, so fitted for the production of melody, is the foremost implement of that effect; but directly the feeling expressed assumes more the character of abstract emotion,—when a broader feeling —the desire to avenge wrong, and to consummate justice, arises,—emphasis becomes the chief power in the effect, and the orchestra take the lead in its production, whilst the voice defines only the salient points of a broad rhythmical design.

The circumstances which beset a musician when entering upon dramatic composition, differ so much from those he meets in the case of any other kind of music that they require a modification of the function generally pertaining to the composer. Both in the case of instrumental and of cantata music, the composer's function is to express emotion as fully and completely as he can, and he is subjected to no conditions but those of a purely musical kind. On the other hand, in the case of dramatic composition, he is surrounded by a framework of external conditions, his office being not simply to enter into an exhaustive expression of this or that emotion, but rather to throw into more or less lengthy expression, a mingled variety of feeling—feeling both transient and deep—as it becomes unfolded in the progress of the piece. Thus, under the former circumstances, the music may at any point, be elaborated to the highest degree, whilst in the latter case, such elaboration can only be introduced at rare intervals. The choice of these intervals amidst the general material and moral circumstances of the piece, should be one of the composers most important considerations.

In laying out the plan for the music of an Opera, the first object, then, should be, to discover those points in the story which are morally appropriate for, and to which the dramatic circumstances will permit, extended musical expression. The music to these points, may be carried to almost any pitch of elaboration, and it will constitute the *backbone* of the whole work. The occasions where this full expression and elaborate construction, may be appropriately introduced, may be described generally as those where sentiment of the instinctive type but of great warmth, and of an elevated order, is unfolded; or where in some important part of the piece, abstract feeling is displayed. Leonora's grand air, in the first act of Beethoven's opera, 'Fidelio,' is an example of the one kind; the prisoner's first chorus, in the same opera, is an example of the other. No occasion could be more appropriate for full musical display than the latter. Here the sentiment to which elaborate expression is given, is an abstract one, namely freedom; and this expression elicits the listener's sympathy with a lofty idea, as well as that narrower sympathy he has with the prisoners personally.*

With respect to the intermediate music, at all those points of the piece where the progress of the plot chiefly elicits interest, the illustration should be as brief as possible; even when in these circumstances a warm flow of feeling occurs, the composer should endeavour to exert a faculty of selection and compression similar to that which I have described Beethoven as having exerted in instrumental composition. With the generality of composers it is much easier to fall into the composition of a graceful melody, as a suggestive passage of their literary text presents itself for illustration, than, by reflecting,

---

* Beautiful as this chorus is, the idea suggests itself to me, that Beethoven might have made more of the occasion—that, here, he might have appropriately given a far fuller and more elaborate expression to the—
    'Eternal spirit of the chainless mind.'

The subdued utterance of the prisoners upon the approach of a guard, is made the occasion for the production of the element of contrast in this chorus: it is a somewhat common-place occasion; but that it is allowed to absorb half the effort of the composition, illustrates the servile way in which even very great composers sometimes adhere to their literary text. Here are two subjects for music:—the idea of liberty, and the fear of some prisoners upon the approach of a guard; and one receives a treatment nearly as elaborate as the other.

G

to catch the essential spirit of this passage, to throw it into terse musical expression, and, in obedience to dramatic exigencies, to reject all other musical promptings. The more perfectly, however, this is done wherever the progress of circumstances chiefly elicits interest, the more dramatic the music will be, and the more effective the general work: but besides these advantages, a great and special musical advantage results. Through the art-space saved by this condensing and culling process, a musician is enabled to illustrate in the greatest power and depth his art and genius are capable of, those salient points of the drama where some heroic human feeling is displayed, or where ideal sentiment arises. On such occasions of this nature as a good librettist might present, I think compositions almost as deep and elaborate as Beethoven's symphonies and Handel's choruses, might be employed. The literary author should, of course, make these occasions,—as in fact every occasion,— arise naturally and necessarily out of the progress of the piece. However great a musical effort may be, if it refers to circumstances not vitally connected with the plot, it is realised in diminished force because it falls upon preoccupied minds, and interrupts, rather than contributes to, the interest and sympathy which fill them. The soldiers' chorus in Gounod's 'Faust,' refers to events that are not closely related to the plot; and however effective this chorus may be, even in these circumstances, it would be doubly effective if it was more judiciously introduced. The coronation march in Meyerbeer's 'Prophète,' on the other hand, refers to a culminating incident of the plot; this music, consequently, possesses both intrinsic and relative interest.

It is the custom of librettists to employ the chorus to set off the expression of personal feeling proper to the principal characters, by uttering its impression of the spectacle. The concluding chorus of Beethoven's 'Fidelio,' is an instance of this practice. This custom has certainly the warrantry of antiquity, as the chorus of the ancient Greek tragedy, was employed in a similar way, its function being that of constantly vibrating between the audience and the persons represented. If, however, the object of the modern drama is 'to hold the mirror up to nature,' the custom above described, should be abandoned except in those cases where the emotion expressed by the principal characters, is of the abstract order; and the chorus should be chiefly used to express abstract emotion. The tendency of large gatherings of men, is to suppress the instinctive, and to give voice to abstract sentiments. On these occasions such ideas as duty, justice, patriotism, &c., are those to which homage is paid; and the feeling these arouse is of the abstract order.* To express this feeling, then, should be considered the grand function of the chorus. At the same time the present custom may be advantageously retained in such scenes as where a chorus is assumed to be sung by peasantry, soldiers, fishermen, people, &c. Although only when the subject-matter of the chorus, is exuberant animal spirits, is it, in these scenes, illustrative of actual life, still, in conjunction with the orchestra, it imparts to them a general life-like animation that could not otherwise be given to them; for few can have failed to experience the unsatisfactory impression such scenes in

* The fact that when the occasion is of a religious nature, the feeling expressed, possesses a more personal character, is an exception to this statement: this kind of occasion is made the subject of remark in the next chapter.

the regular drama, give, especially when they are sustained for some length of time.

The reader may have observed that thus far in this work, no emotion has been referred to but that of an healthy kind,—no mention having been made of evil feeling. But the choice of literary subjects, displayed in the case of several modern operas, implies that music may be employed to express this feeling also. The modern doctrine of evil in man is, that it is a negative condition, and arises when certain natural impulses ordained for our benefit, escape uncontrolled through the absence of other conditions; that, as the yielding to violent passion, often denotes physical infirmity, so all bad acts and feelings, arise through some combination of physical, mental, and moral shortcomings; briefly, that the bad man has not too much, but too little. This being so, when evil is chosen for the subject-matter of art, her fine and intense light, instead of being made to shine upon a phenomenon wherein the powers of nature tend to formation, strength, usefulness, goodness, or beauty, is thrown upon a process of dissolution; and all that it can catch to irradiate, are some of those fleeing elements of virtue which alone ever give character and energy to evil. Where the artist seizes some of these elements, his assumed expression of evil may possess true force as in the case of Milton's Satan; but where evil,—it being assumed to be a positive quality,—is endeavoured to be grasped, no effect is consummated, as in the cases of Moore's Mokanna, and Shelley's Count Cenci. Toward the end of this chapter, I shall glance at the broad reason why we cannot admire art unless it breathes a spirit of goodness. In the meantime, by the fact that this negative phenomenon, evil, like physical disease, produces in the regarder, a feeling of revulsion, it is easy to show that it cannot inspire music. It is noticeable that in life an allowed evil fact is never the subject of eloquence; that, on the other hand, eloquence is generally inspired by something admirable. The reason of this is, that when an influence produces a pleasant impression in us, our first impulse is to try and sustain this impression; and, as when an influence pleases us through the eye, we continue to gaze, or try to reproduce it by painting it, so, when the agreeable influence is a fact of life, or anything producing the inward emotion of admiration, we recount it, analyse it, and enlarge all we can in our expression of it, in order that the emotion it produces, may be sustained both by the mind continuing to dwell on this influence and by sympathy with its effect on others.* But when an influence produces an unpleasant feeling in us, our first impulse is to try to get rid of the feeling. Music then, cannot be inspired by evil because the mind, refusing to dwell on the pure morbid aspect of the phenomenon, the feeling it produces is not sustained; indeed, it appears on the surface, unlikely, that where the object is pleasure, we should endeavour voluntarily to retain a species of feeling which we try involuntarily to get rid of because it is unpleasant. Thus it is, that when a composer endeavours to express evil feeling, he either expresses only its apparent energy, thus producing more or less true effect, or else he unconsciously testifies to the negativeness of evil, by relinquishing altogether the task of expression, and

* This is the nature of the impulse which gives rise to the principle of *representation*. See page 15.

exhibiting the opposite of music—harsh discord and distorted melody.

There are considerations which suggest that present emotional pain is, also, a subject which a musical composer cannot illustrate. This subject occurs in Meyerbeer's opera, 'Le Prophète,' in which Jean of Leyden's short agony of indecision upon being compelled to sacrifice his betrothed or see his mother killed, is one of the principal points. In real life a person enduring the actual pang of mental pain, is generally undemonstrative. It is probable that at such a moment, the nature is almost wholly absorbed in the act of attention to a new and terrible fact; that it does not realise, much less demonstrate the emotions which the fact is calculated to arouse; and that those emotions arise only subsequently. If this is so, then a musician, like Nature, can do nothing, because for the time during which emotion is unrealised, there exists no subject-matter for music to express. It is noticeable that even the poet,—who for giving expression to such an occasion as this, has the advantage of being able to use physical accessories of feeling,—when picturing a character in present emotional pain, generally has recourse to the suggestion of negative traits. For instance thus Parisina after hearing the doom of Hugo, is described—

> 'Her eyes unmoved, but full and wide,
> Not once had turned to either side—
> Nor once did those sweet eyelids close,
> Or shade the glance o'er which they rose,'
> * * * * *

and thus Kaled before Lara's fatal charge:—

> 'His lip was silent, scarcely beat his heart,'

and thus Constance de Beverley before the conclave:—

> 'And there she stood so calm and pale,
> That, but her breathing did not fail,
> And motion slight of eye and head,
> And of her bosom, warranted,
> That neither sense nor pulse she lacks,
> You must have thought a form of wax,
> Wrought to the very life, was there—
> So still she was,' * * *

and thus the demeanour of Macduff at the moment when he is told of the slaughter of his wife and children, is alluded to:—

> *Mal.*   'Merciful heaven!—
> What, man! ne'er pull your hat upon your brows;
> Give sorrow words.' * * * *

Although the passionate demonstration of natural feeling can be vividly expressed by music, there are reasons why it should be sparingly introduced in an opera.

In the first place the principle of generally conforming art to life, suggests this course. In life, whereas abstract feeling generally makes a person enthusiastic, healthy instinctive feeling when unattended by exceptional circumstances, is comparatively undemonstrative. In the second place music inspired by natural feeling in its normal phase, is likely to possess a fuller spirit than music which is animated by this feeling in a passionate phase, for whereas in the latter case natural feeling strikingly but almost exclusively, displays the qualities of strength and warmth; in the former, whilst impressing these qualities, it exhibits also those of sweetness and tenderness : this is, in fact, an exemplification of the truth, now generally recognised by the art-mind, that the qualities of nature, existing more evenly and in more variety in her normal phases than in her convulsions, a richer art inspiration may be drawn from her under the former than under the latter circumstances. As another illustration of this, it may be observed that whereas the spectacle of a volcanic eruption, or of an earthquake, impresses chiefly the ideas of power and confusion, an upright shoot of grass impresses the ideas of power, repose, organization, and beauty; thus the latter object is the richer in suggestiveness. In the third place, it will be observed that the exhibition of feeling,—whether instinctive or abstract,—in a calm condition, can be more easily regarded in a disinterested personal spirit, than its exhibition in a passionate state can be; and that when thus regarded, the sympathy aroused, is sympathy for the abstract beauty of the emotion. But a forcible display of feeling, will generally cause a regarder to forget his position as a contemplator, to feel a strong personal interest in, and to sympathise in a special way with, the spectacle. Now as in life, in the case of each individual, the objects of instinctive feeling are special and limited,—as they can only consist of friends and relatives,—it is plain, supposing that the above spectacle consists of this feeling, that certain emotional chords in the regarder might be struck, which in life can only truly vibrate to one touch, and that the feeling thus aroused must be hollow and artificial. On the other hand, as the scope of abstract feeling is broad and unlimited,—as, for instance, such a feeling as the love of liberty may vibrate truly to innumerable touches,—it is also plain, supposing that the above spectacle consists of abstract feeling, that the sympathy of the regarder would always be of a genuine character. Although, then, the exhibition of instinctive feeling in a calm and natural state, when it is regarded as an object of contemplation, may edify, its representation in a passionate state and in the average stage of development, is, at least, purposeless,—for instance, what advantage can there be in a strong accession of artificial brotherly, sisterly, or parental feeling in just that stage of development in which everybody realises these feelings? At the same time, it should be observed, that in those rare instances where feelings of this nature, are represented beyond the average stage of development,—as being purer and finer than they are in society,—their exhibition, whether in a passionate state or not, is, in several important ways edifying. It may appear that the whole weight of custom—of the example of the greatest dramatists and writers, bears against the spirit of these remarks. We must remember, however, that this custom descends from the remote past, and may have originated in times and circumstances when the natural sentiments were dull, and little more spiritual than animal instincts—when lofty domestic virtues were rare. In these circumstances, the representation of instinctive sentiments in vivid warmth and in delicate phases, would tend to unlock in the hearts of the spectators, the avenues to the purer and tenderer development of these feelings; and the exhibition of lofty domestic virtues, would be highly salutary. We may conclude then, that only when this order of feeling is exhibited in such an advanced stage of development, as to apply to present life in the way above described, is its passionate display either morally or intellectually beneficial to the spectator.

The deep but concealed devotion of Leonora in Beethoven's opera, 'Fidelio,' is an example of instinctive sentiment introduced in an opera in general accordance with these remarks. This love is not simply warm, tender, passively pure and faithful, but it embraces the qualities of active devotedness and heroic courage. Thus it is in a stage of development beyond that in which it ordinarily exists, or in which it is ordinarily seen to exist. Yet even this feeling is sparingly demonstrated,—the fire seldom flames, though it is ever felt to be glowing beneath protracted and nobly self contained action,—only when the climax of the plot arrives, is it exhibited without restraint.

I have previously argued that music characterised by elaborate and strongly marked rhythm should attend the expression of abstract sentiment, on the ground that similar effects in a rudimentary form attend the demonstration of the same order of feeling, in language,—this being the shape in which, in life, we meet the fact, that abstract sentiment is enthusiastic; and that this principle should be observed in a drama—in circumstances where the art-intention is to catch the spirit of life, is obvious. On the ground of truthfulness to nature, and on the ground of expediency,—which in art-matters always coincides with that of truthfulness to nature,—I have also argued that music should chiefly express instinctive sentiment in its full but comparatively silent flow; that energetic expressions of this feeling should, if ever, be sparingly introduced.

Now if we continue still further our observation of life, we find that not only is instinctive sentiment rarely and slightly demonstrated, but that important abstract sentiment, though demonstrated enthusiastically when demonstrated at all, is only exhibited at comparatively rare intervals; that, in short, the more continuous occupation of the mind and the demonstrative faculties, is neither the one action nor the other, but the expression of that minor abstract sentiment which attends the enlightened observation of the lesser truths and beauties of the world. The secondary part of the subject-matter of a musical drama should, therefore, consist chiefly of this sentiment and idea. This kind of subject-matter is, at present, to some extent introduced in operas, as when one of the characters apostrophises the seasons, night, flowers, &c.; or when a choral ode to labour, rest, leisure, or peace, &c., is sung. The questions, however, I think are worthy of some consideration, whether for such occasions as these, more originality and variety, as regards subject, might not be attained; and whether they might not be extended so as to fill some of that art-space now occupied by matter which appeals to the instinctive feelings. A keen discrimination and tender sympathy, animating a librettist, might discover many gleams of beauty in every-day life, fit to form the subject of music, and the exhibition of which in the circumstances of the musical drama, would be salutary. Those minor incidents of life which suggest reflection; the beauty of common and humble objects; that which is pure and high in every-day thought, and fragrant in small actions, are materials from which true art-inspiration may be drawn: that the greatest in art have exemplified this fact, and that it holds good in the dramatic form of art, the instance and example of Shakespeare are a sufficient proof. But it may be said that comments more or less poetical or philosophical, sometimes argumentative, at others, satirical, on every-day life, will not with any advantage, bear musical effect. There is, it is true, an order of verbal statement that gains no advantage from being accompanied with music, and, therefore, which is better without it; this is statement of which the utterance and reception are generally unattended by emotion, such as the expression of incidental material fact, or of highly abstract truth, like mathematical truth,—statement of either so low a character, or so divested of human association, as not to elicit sympathy. This order of statement may be more comprehensively described, as statement of which the object and influence,—however important may be the one, and impressive the other,—are not the production of emotions of any kind. But I need scarcely say that a good author would not introduce much matter of this kind into a work so closely related to the sphere of poetry as the drama is. In Shakespeare's plays, for instance, if we except the humorous scenes, we find, without taking into account the markedly serious ones, that the language in almost every line, 'extracts emotions beautiful and new.' That the literary basis of the intermediate or secondary music of operas, might be far richer in ideas, far more original, and of a considerably higher moral tone than it is in most cases at present, cannot be doubted.

The proposition that music may be devised to aid

the expression of important thought, will not appear, *primâ facie*, unnatural to the reader, as I have previously pointed out that in this expression by language, rudimentary effects of one of the essential elements of music, naturally arise; nor will this proposition appear improbable, supposing my assumption is correct, that the emotion attendant upon thought, constitutes a high and most important part of the field of musical inspiration. But if music can be inspired by the feeling which attends thought, we may assume as a general truth, that it may advantageously attend the verbal expression of thought, if we may be guided by a fact in analogous circumstances, it being indisputable that music may not only be inspired by instinctive feeling but may advantageously attend the verbal expression of this feeling. Language which expresses thought, is of course appropriate in different degrees for being attended by music; and some of it is inappropriate.

Important thought may be defined as that action of the mind by which we arrive at the perception and appreciation of certain new truths, or of ideas submitted as truths : that which animates music in these circumstances, is the emotion aroused by the truths and ideas which strike the attention in the course, and at the climax, of this action. Now in the degree that the more mechanical operation of the mind,— the pure reasoning,—is simple in proportion to the greatness and emotional suggestiveness of the truths and ideas that form its subject, will it be possible for the language that is involved, to be advantageously attended by music: where the reasoning is very elaborate and the truth unsuggestive, the language may be pronounced unfit for music; where the reasoning is moderately elaborate and the truth great, the language might be wrought by the aid of music, into an expression of the highest and most effective kind; where the truth is great and the more mechanical operation of the mind, is slight, the language will be generally best fitted for music, as the development of the pure musical expression will be in these circumstances least likely to be hampered by the often necessary incorporation of irrelevant words.* As in the case of any literary episode that has been already

* The lingual construction best adapted for music, is considered in the following chapter.

set to music, it may be observed that various portions are adapted for musical illustration in different degrees, and that they accordingly bear musical effects more or less full, so that order of language which I have indicated as generally fitted to form the subject of musical expression, of course, is fitted to do this in different degrees; and to well prepare a literary episode for music, besides an observance of the principles above laid down, a fine exercise of judgment and even much experiment,—resulting in a further work of selection and rejection,—will be, doubtless, always necessary.

The idea that music can aid the verbal expression of thought in the drama, not only is not generally entertained but is often ridiculed: this is frequently done by allusion being made to the case of music participating in the enunciation of the soliloquies of a Hamlet. The confident spirit in which such allusions as this, are made, is really an evidence of how little this art has been philosophically investigated, and of how one-sided its development has been hitherto: on the stage its development has not been even one-sided, for here music's function has been chiefly to endow commonplace and frivolous circumstances with a power and beauty of effect, to supply inanimate language with earnestness of spirit. We may as reasonably assume that music can be inspired by that feeling which is behind thought and even the utterance of thought, as that it can be inspired by instinctive feeling. The fact of the depth and seriousness of the emotional impressure which fine instrumental music creates, suggests that there is a close sympathy between music and the emotional state attendant upon an elevated frame of mind. That music may be linked to the utterance of thought, even experience shows; it is felt in the case of the oratorio, to aid in a strikingly effective way, the enunciation of passages of the grandest poetical character, and which sprang out of thought as elevated and as far removed from the commonplace and frivolous, as thought can possibly be. On the stage, the experiment of uniting music with thoughtful utterance, has not been so frequently tried as for it to be safe to conclude that it necessarily entails failure. Gounod's musical investiture of Faust's opening soliloquy,—which is still the utterance of thought, though the utterance is passionate, and the thought, morbid,—rather suggests the opposite conclusion.

It will be observed that the principles I have laid down in this and the preceding chapters, are based upon facts of life. Some, it is true, apply to the subject only in a very broad way, and others, are of a negative character. Yet if they only serve to impress composers with the fact that music is a thing that rests on life, they will not prove unprofitable; for, as I shall now proceed to show, life is the source of what is true and highest in the spirit of art, and of what is most efficacious in its form.

Arts such as music and the drama, the chief animating principle of which, is human feeling, must draw their spirit from life, or they cannot possibly give us elevated pleasure, because our very conception of what is admirable in feeling, is drawn from life; in fact, our conceptions of all the higher qualities relating to the spirit or form of art, and which we refer to by the terms, beautiful, sublime, dignified, &c., have been nurtured and trained in the atmosphere of life. We may, I think, regard as truths the following statements:—that a people has always prospered in the degree that it has practised virtue: * that as in the case of individuals, much experience of life, generally tends to give, or to considerably strengthen, an impression of the necessity and advantage of virtue, so the experience of peoples, establishes in the general mind the same impression: that, thus, individual experience, combined with the practical lessons taught by the past, causes a people to regard moral virtue as one of its vital features: and that this habit of mind prevailing throughout generations, causes the feeling of respect for virtue to become almost an instinct. Thus it is, that each individual, be he good or bad, of a people that has emerged from barbarism, inevitably possesses some respect for virtue; and in the same way, a people that by its virtues, has attained a somewhat elevated life—that has risen to the enjoyment of peace, and to the perception of some of the beauty and light of life, necessarily and intuitively pays homage to those

* 'The earliest phenomenon likely to be observed connected with the moral government of the world is the general one, that on the whole, as things are constituted, good men prosper and are happy, bad men fail and are miserable.'—J. A. FROUDE, *on the Book of Job*.

feelings and principles of action which have led to its advancement: thus we admire righteousness, goodness, love, and whatever we consider virtue. Moreover, this feeling of the excellence and beauty of virtue, is the fundamental feeling of our life; it mingles with and influences all other feelings; apart from it we never feel earnestly about anything; it is in fact that which gives warmth to all other feelings: directly it is opened up, warmth comes. Thus, whenever we feel earnestly, we are not only conscious of being right, but we feel that we have morally advanced through the fact of our emotion. So closely is the idea of virtue associated with earnest feeling of any kind, that when we speak generally of a person as having betrayed feeling, we imply that at the time he had either an accession to his character of some good element, or that a former latent element of virtue in him, was then awakened.* Thus it is that

---

* This proposition, that a feeling only becomes warm as it raises the fundamental feeling of respect and admiration for virtue, reminds me of the following statement which is from an important modern work:—
'No heart is pure that is not passionate.' The reader will observe that these propositions supplement one-another. The former being to the effect that all warm feeling must be to some extent, virtuous, leaves untouched the question whether other than warm feeling can be virtuous:

true music being always inspired by vivid and warm emotion, inevitably breathes a spirit of goodness or impresses us with a sense of its presence. This goes some way to explain that strong sympathy between music and the human heart, which has struck the attention of men from the earliest times, and also that relation between sensibility to music and virtuous susceptibility, to which Shakespeare has alluded.

As, then, the love and admiration of virtue, is our strongest feeling, so, whatever other qualities of music elicit our admiration, the expression which it possesses by reason of the warmth and virtue of the feeling by which it is animated, always constitutes the strength of its charm: music, then, appeals chiefly to a faculty of admiration which practical life has developed. Thus

but to the question whether other than warm feeling can be *highly* virtuous, the latter proposition is an answer in the negative. Again, the latter proposition being to the effect that highly virtuous feeling must be warm, leaves untouched the question whether other than highly virtuous feeling, can be warm: but to the question whether other than feeling *to some extent virtuous*, can be warm, the former proposition is an answer in the negative. Thus the propositions taken jointly, betray a closer relation between the qualities, warmth and purity with reference to feeling, than is betrayed by either proposition, taken singly, the joint effect of both being, that no other than warm feeling can be highly virtuous, and that no other than feeling to some extent virtuous, can be warm.

the simple fact of music moving the feelings to genuine awe or admiration—filling us with a fervent sense of moral beauty, is a proof that such music is animated in an important degree by some moral element in life—that it rests upon a foundation of truth.

This tendency to pay homage to what has proved serviceable to humanity, is manifested in the case of service of all kinds. Nor is it simply the idea of morality to which homage is paid, but the various forms and institutions through which it is fostered and administered, as well as the implements employed, are also held in honour: this is shown in the respect which is so generally accorded to government, law, religion and schools, and to the soldier, the statesman, the priest, and the teacher. And the respect arising on this principle, extends to almost everything, small, or great, in life. Everything associated with virtuous labour and the feelings of practical life, commands in some degree our respect, or admiration; and the most humble thing possessing this association, is held in higher honour than the most extensive thing that has it not. The smallest relic which relates to some necessary or serviceable function of past life, possesses a pathos and dignity, and elicits a far higher respect than even a pyramid, or any wanton achievement, however vast.

As, then, we are only moved by the spirit of art when this spirit is drawn from life, and our faculties have been moulded by it, so we always admire the form of art most when it wears the likeness of material life, and therefore of something that our faculties have been educated to respect. This is why all art the form of which is the imagery of life,—such as sculpture, painting, poetry, and the drama,—is considered, *primâ facie*, by the generality of people, to possess the quality of dignity in a higher degree than music. Our very conceptions of the qualities, dignity, importance, &c., have been moulded by the standard of the necessary and serviceable in life; and the relation of music to life, not being palpably visible in its form, its claims to respect are naturally not felt by those who are not moved by its spirit.

Our conceptions of the various qualities of art being, then, drawn from life, faithfulness to life in the spirit, and where possible, in the form, of art, is the key to admiration, which is the arbiter of art. Thus, principles of construction based upon facts of life, are a sound foundation for art, and some importance may be seen to attach to the principles I have laid down with reference to the use of the accentuated and melodic forms of music, the circumstances attending the composition of instrumental music, the employment of the chorus, the general forms and degrees of expression to be given to abstract and instinctive sentiment in an opera, the character and conformation of its literary matter—what should prevail and what be rejected. Unless music is animated by feeling it occupies the same art-level as a geometrical design: whereas, however, it is always apparent by the form of his art, whether a painter intended to express high emotion, or to please merely the sense, it is not so in the case of music—particularly instrumental. Through the form of music being apparently unrelated to life, its chief function, which is the expression of emotion, is but loosely associated with instrumental music. As, then, the principles I have laid down, imply that to some extent music even in form, is based on life, these principles may benefit instrumental music indirectly, if they remind the composer of its general relation to life, and thus of the higher function which pertains to it.

If it be true that moral energy though unresolved into definite feelings, may set in motion the musical faculty, we must bear in mind that even this kind of art-impulse is the sense of an emotional capacity which has been greatly developed and conformed through the previous life-experience of humanity: and it is not less true, as I shall endeavour to show in the next chapter, that music is always fine in the degree that the emotion animating it, has been strongly and definitely felt.

The broad field of life is the fresh source of all high and healthy emotion whether arising from human relation, thought, contemplation of nature, or from sympathy with the experience of others. Life not only elicits but strengthens and purifies feeling; it is the crucible in which emotion is tested, and out of which all that is true must come. As in the case of an individual, certain feelings may be implanted during youth, but life can alone test them and bring them to strength, so of all feeling it may be said that the fresher it comes from life the stronger and purer it is. Thus it is that primitive melodies,—airs which have been inspired by feeling fresh from life—pressed out by the actual circumstances of life, possess an originality, vigour, freshness, and sweetness of expression, that time cannot take from them. Arising out of warm, unaffected feeling, they command sympathy, and being rooted in a portion of the living truth of the world, they are felt to be as unique and unsurpassable as nature's wild flowers. This music is ever fresh because it sprang from true and living feeling; whilst so much of the writings of professional musicians, has passed to oblivion, because it was more the expression of taste, or skill, or of the musical learning, form, and fashion of its day than of any real moral afflatus. The general truths these observations imply are: first, that true feeling is indispensable for the production of music: secondly, that the form of music should spring out of the nature and circumstances of the emotion which inspires it, forcible effects being unmeaning unless they are the expression of enthusiastic feeling, whilst the construction of elaborate forms, unless they are the expression of broad and important feeling, or unless the object is practice, is but ingenious trifling. Briefly, for genuine inspiration and the production of original and enduring music, the composer must in the words of Robert Schuman, 'Look deeply into life, and study it as diligently as the other arts and sciences.'

CHAPTER VI.

THE SPIRIT OF SACRED MUSIC.—REMARKS ON THE ORATORIO.

THE intention of sacred music, is the expression of abstract and instinctive feeling united. The conception of a divine Creator and Father, gives to all incentives of feeling to be found in creation, the character of works of intelligence and providence, and thus imparts to man's sympathy for whatsoever is grand and beautiful in nature, the definiteness and heartfelt warmth of personal sympathy. An emotional phenomenon is here involved in which abstract feeling possesses the warmth and concentrated energy of instinctive feeling, and in which the latter feeling possesses the broad and lofty scope and permanent vitality of intellectual sympathy; into which, moreover, enter those yearnings and aspirations general in man for fuller and higher existence.

Through a peculiarity of the modern mind, this condition of feeling has been prevented entering in its entirety, the conceptions of composers of sacred music; it is, however, the typical spirit of this music, and is largely present in it. From this spirit sacred music catches those remarkable combinations of high qualities, grandeur and earnestness, majesty and tenderness, austerity and pathos.

It is a curious fact that man should have artificially exercised into separate action two great casts of thought and feeling, namely the strictly serious and moral cast, and the more poetical and philosophical one; that he should have two general lights of survey. It might be reasonably supposed that the admission of religion into his sphere of truth, would have rather tended to impart entireness than partiality, to the spirit of his survey. Nevertheless, perhaps among other causes,*

---

* 'Thus, no system of law, or articles of belief were or could be complete and exhaustive for all time. Experience accumulates; new facts are observed, new forms display themselves, and all such formulæ must necessarily be from period to period broken up and moulded afresh. And yet the steps already gained are a treasure so sacred, so liable are they at all times to be attacked by those lower and baser elements in our nature which it is their business to hold in check, that the better part of mankind have at all times practically regarded their creed as a sacred total to which nothing may be added, and from which nothing may be taken away.' * * * —J. A. FROUDE, *on the Book of Job.*

owing to the changing of religion in the mind, from a strong literal belief to a more formal tenet; and to that ecclesiastical spirit which has been aimed to exclude from religious conceptions the influence of new mental and emotional growth, it has become the custom to regard everything separately in these two lights, the sacred and the secular. Thus art is separated into two general departments corresponding with man's two lights of survey; the effect of this in the case of music, is to narrow and impoverish both departments. It is true that as up to a certain point the church favored culture generally, it benefited musical art by not only encouraging the growth of more elaborate forms than could have flourished supported only by popular taste but by surrounding music with a high moral atmosphere, and supplying it with a burden both serious and truly poetic; still, as with culture so with music, the plant once grown strong, was no longer nourished by the atmosphere in which it was reared. It cannot fail to be observed, that since the period of Handel music has developed in the secular department, in a greater ratio than in the sacred. Whereas in the former, new forms have arisen, as, for instance, the symphony, and old ones have become more perfectly developed, as in the case of the opera, in the latter, the forms have not increased; whilst what newness of expression sacred music has unfolded in this time, is chiefly the reflection of new idioms which in the first place arose in secular music. Again the habit of partial survey to which I have alluded, has tended to deprive secular music of the deep inspiration of man's more serious conceptions. By referring to a few instances of the inequality which a composer generally betrays when he works respectively in the two styles in question, we may see both the advantages and disadvantages the circumscribed inspiration of the sacred style entails. The secular music of Handel is distinguished by a delicate melody, massiveness, and an austere grandeur; and it is always tasteful and perspicuous; but his sacred music possesses a pathos and sublimity so deep that we cannot conceive that any effect can impress these qualities in a greater degree. Mendelssohn's secular music is intellectual, massive, and elegant; yet it gives the impression that the feeling underlying it was somewhat weakly felt and artificial; it is more sentimental than pathetic, more rhapsodical than eloquent; but his sacred music equals that of Handel in elevated expression though not in power and majesty of effect.* On the other hand, Beethoven has given to his instrumental works a greater fulness and as great a depth of expression, with an equal power and dignity of effect, as any other composer has given to sacred works. But Beethoven was cramped by the sacred forms; in his case the force of inspiration could not be increased by the religious suggestiveness which is here directly met, but was checked by it, by reason of a certain narrowness by which, notwithstanding its loftiness, it is characterised.

The partial survey to which I have alluded, is to a great extent absent from the Bible and the Liturgy

---

* We here see again illustrated the ultimate dependence of musical expression, upon mental exercise. As a rule composers who have been great in secular music, where the ideas they have met, are for the most part unimportant ones, and where, in the case of instrumental music, they have been left to their own imaginations, have become greater in the atmosphere of religion, where massive and lofty ideas present themselves. If music does not depend upon feeling in defined forms for its inspiration, it can only proceed from the energy and the capacity by which what is admirable is conceived and appreciated; and it would appear that the more positively these faculties are exerted by a composer, the greater is his music.

of the English Church. The writers of these works appear to have had but one inclusive spirit of survey; this is evidenced by the philosophic spirit, breadth of thought, poetry and dignity, by which they are distinguished. But when references are made to Scripture in the present day, whether for a devotional or an artistic purpose, it is customary to leave out of sight the general world of suggestiveness—to exclude from the occasion, the influence of new mental growth and new phases of feeling. Except in the case of the more advanced intellects, religious conceptions are regarded from a past position of the mind, and not as the sacred writers regarded them, from its natural position in the present. For instance, in the general mind, the idea of an intelligent Source of all phenomena, does not mingle freely with the stream of suggestiveness pouring from nature and life, in the same way that a certain natural truth is always realised subject to the influence of others. This idea realised freely, would embrace all that is high and beautiful in the suggestiveness of the natural world; yet as generally realised, its principal attributes are omnipotence and mingled mercifulness and austerity, many high qualities being not only absent, but their absence is another and not the least important attribute. It is probable that during the time when the early conceptions of this idea were formed, the faculty of wielding power in the broad forms of creation and destruction, reward and punishment, was the most elevated and majestic quality that nature and life had suggested, and that the mind could conceive. Thus, although mingling freely with all the suggestiveness that reached the mind, this idea was then naturally enrobed in this limited range of attributes. But, unfortunately, this is its present form in the general mind. We can here imagine how disadvantageous it is for art, for the ideas that inspire it, to be realised from a past position of the mind. It is also undesirable for modern ideas to be expressed in ancient forms of art. The change which has taken place in the form and spirit of music since Handel's time; which is visible in new melodic and harmonic effects, more frequent modulation, and more varied expression, seems at first sight, to have rendered the modern style less fitted than the more ancient, to express religious ideas. There is little doubt that the latter is the better, for expressing the idea to which I have already alluded, as it is popularly realised. To express a conception of which eternity, changelessness, power, and holiness, are almost the sole associations, demands a condition of art tending to massiveness and simplicity, not to variety and delicacy of idiom. But 'changelessness in the midst of change' cannot remain an attribute of this idea, whatever may be the nature of the Truth for which it stands. This, with all other conceptions of the unknown, must be ever undergoing modification— ever approaching truth, as the suggestiveness pouring in upon the mind and sympathy, gets richer and deeper. Consequently, the most recent development of musical, as of all art—the condition which reflects most faithfully all the ideas and feelings that nature and life have created in the breast—the condition richest in expression, must be the more appropriate for expressing that idea which the poet Thompson in an intellectual spirit, calls, ' the varied God.'

The highly beneficial influence the church has had upon music in having supplied it with definite and lofty subjects, tends to put out of sight the disadvantages an arbitrarily circumscribed suggestiveness entails. And we are the less likely to see anything but the advantages which have resulted from the connection of the church with music, on account of the fact that secular music in so many cases, has been grafted upon comparatively unimportant ideas. The general conclusions to which these considerations point are:—that progressiveness of form and expression cannot unfold in a department of art whose source of inspiration only embraces particular eras of history and of the mind—from which the direct inspiration of nature is excluded; that although the conventionally circumscribed religious channel of suggestiveness, has given great and needful inspiration to music, it is not alone a sufficiently broad foundation for a progressive school of composition; and that the general art conditions which beset secular composition, are the more favorable for the expression of that spirit of inspiration suggested at the opening of this chapter.* Beethoven who drew deep poetic feelings from nature, religion, and his own intellectual life, has united the earnest-

* There is a peculiar propriety in the chorus entering largely into music inspired by this order of feeling. Its power of marked emphasis: of assuming the fugal form; and that quality of expression it has through being the effect of human voices, tend to closely adapt it to express emotion compounded of both abstract and instinctive feeling.

ness, depth, and grandeur of the sacred school, with the fulness, poetry, and variety, of the secular. Truths do not naturally present themselves to the mind in the conventional order to which I have referred. In broad deliberation the suggestiveness from all points of the mental landscape, tends to blend. It may be said on the other hand, that as the art-mind is sensitive to the beautiful and great in all forms, when it applies itself to the expression of religious formulæ, this broad sympathy must speak, and that thus in sacred musical works, there is to be met that fulness of expression just alluded to. Whereas, however, when broad religious feeling is expressed in secular forms, it meets the fuller resources and natural idioms, when expressed in sacred forms, it meets the more restricted resources and arbitrarily preserved idioms. Still, it is probable that a highly comprehensive order of emotion does become expressed in church music. In the musical enlarging upon those definite and grand ideas which a church formula involves, there probably enters much of that suggestiveness which, recruited by new truth and new ideas, is ever flowing to the mind of man, and forming and modifying feeling; thus the music may be animated by a broader spirit than that in which its literary text is used. There can be little doubt that with the change now fast coming over religious thought, the partial habit of mind I have spoken of will disappear; that what is fundamental in religious feeling, will be strengthened by the light as it enters more into daily life and leavens all other feelings; and that the sacred style of music, will thus become more broadly based on truth, and consequently more beautiful.

I speak of the oratorio under the heading of sacred music for convenience. Although it is an offshoot of this style, and contains both its virtues and faults, I regard it as a free form. For it to be a reasonable one two of its present features must disappear: namely, its subjects being drawn exclusively from the Bible, and its dramatic form. Whatever arguments might be raised for the retention of the former feature, so long as the oratorio is considered a sacred form of art, cannot apply to it as a free form. At the same time, it may be presumed that its subject would still embrace the highest conceptions of the human mind, whether conceived in the past or shaped in the light of present knowledge; that it would be drawn generally from high poetical and moral writing.

A very unreasonable practice in connection with music, is that of adopting for the subject of cantatas, literature which contains no important ideas, and whose only pretence to character, exists in virtue of its bearing a weak impress of the drama. If a drama is too weak to bear action, scenic and histrionic effect, it is unworthy of musical illustration as a drama. In the case of an effective drama, where the characters and sentiments have a strong complexion of reality, only a great composer can attain graphic expression, or exhibit the true dramatic faculty, namely, that of feeling strongly the spirit of the occasion. How difficult, then, must be the composer's task where the characters are shadowy, and the sentiments unoriginal! These objections apply to the oratorio, which is a copy of the drama, in so far as it consists of a long dialogue and a group of characters, yet is without action, the appearance of reality, or an interesting plot; and although it embraces ideas so weighty as to reward undivided attention, these do not strengthen it as a drama, they only serve to give it other standing-ground. Now I think it may be presumed, that instead of the subjects of the cantata and oratorio, consisting in the one case of a chain of common-place sentiments enunciated by shadowy characters, and in the other, of transcriptions from the Bible, in a faintly dramatic form, they should not be specially distinguished by characters or plot at all, but by ideas and imagery. The 'Messiah' and 'Israel in Egypt' are the two greatest oratorios; the character and form of their subjects, are essential causes of this superiority; and in neither is there any attempt to copy the drama. In neither is there dialogue, characters, or plot, in the dramatic sense; but throughout both works there is an uninterrupted moral progressiveness,—a development less of incidents than of ideas. The former work is a graphic expression of the spirit of Christianity, and of the character and attributes of its Founder; each *air*, *chorus*, and *recitative*, gives new development to this exalted subject; and the progressiveness being purely of a moral character, a comprehensive interest is elicited at each stage. As a contrast to this, remark the subject of Mendelssohn's 'Elijah.' This being in the dramatic form, elicits chiefly interest of an incidental and personal character; and the progressiveness being chiefly circumstantial, the ideas that meet the attention at its different stages, are of very uneven elevation. It being customary for the composer of an oratorio to permit himself full expression at each point of the work, gives these considerations additional importance. A subject fitted for elaborate treatment at all points, should at each, elicit a wide interest; and one whose chief feature is an impress of the ordinary drama, cannot do this. It is also obvious that music which is elaborated to an equal degree at many points, is particularly undramatic. In 'Israel in Egypt' a series of catastrophes is described, on such a scale as to produce impressions more akin to epic poetry than the drama, the subject being a progressive exemplification of the powerful interposition of Jehovah. I would, then, point to the books of the 'Messiah' and 'Israel in Egypt' as models of the more appropriate style of literature for oratorios. To recapitulate, the chief features of this style are:—freedom; intellectual and moral rather than personal and incidental progressiveness; and uniform comprehensiveness, a feature which would naturally result from that of moral progressivness. It is apparent in the case of this order of literature, that all necessity for the ordinary dramatic element for an incentive of inspiration, is superseded.

Music set to language is generally more perspicuous than pure instrumental music, not only because it is technically but, to some extent, because it is morally simpler. Although words and sounds are closely related, it is to be remembered that they belong to different principles of demonstration. The former suggest stereotyped feelings through their names, and more complex feelings through the description of attending circumstances, whereas the latter are not symbols, and they cannot indicate material phenomena. When an emotion is alluded to in language, any important single word either refers to some accessory of the feeling, and thus suggests it very imperfectly, or not at all; or else it is the name of a complete feeling, and might inspire a musical movement. We here see that the various feelings which may be implied by a certain passage of language, cannot be adequately expressed by music if a certain measure of sounds has to coincide with the same measure of syllables or words; and why music in the form of the ballad or psalm-tune, seldom has the fulness of expression which music to unmeasured words generally possesses. Terse language containing a few important sentiments, is, thus, the best for music: in these circumstances a composer can express a feeling in various phases without having to incorporate words referring to subordinate and sometimes trifling ideas, which attend more or less necessarily all ordinary language, and eke out metrical literature; he has neither to curtail the development of a broad feeling of inspiration in order to find room for a more weakly felt piece of effect nor to connect music inspired by an important anterior sentiment, with subsequent language that has no connection with it. The outward connection between music and words is often a forced one; and often when in one place it is real, in another, it is unreal. These considerations help to explain the marked superiority of the music of the 'Messiah' and 'Israel in Egypt' to that of Handel's other oratorios. The language of the former works being drawn bodily from the English Bible, is a terse and graphic expression of grand and broad sentiments; whereas that of the latter works, is metrical, and the production of second-rate poets. The grand effect of the 'Hallelujah chorus' would scarcely have been possible with metrical language—if the few simple but weighty phrases of its text, were expanded with unessential matter.

CHAPTER VII.

SOME REMARKS CONCERNING THE INFLUENCE OF MENTAL PROGRESS UPON MUSIC.—CONCLUSION.

INSTINCTIVE sentiment is greatly influenced by mental progress, though in a less degree than abstract sentiment. The latter order of feeling may be changed entirely in the course of a great advance of the mind; for instance, the conception of a Creator, which in a barbaric time is associated chiefly with the feeling of fear, becomes under the influence of enlightenment associated with feeling of an almost opposite kind. The former, though not subject to changes so radical as this, may still undergo considerable modification, becoming more comprehensive and finer, as society advances; and it should be added, that if enlightenment never changes entirely a personal feeling, it calls new ones into life; for example, it is said that the feelings of duty, honor, and friendship, do not exist in very early stages of society.

If we compare the domestic sentiments of the present day, with the same kind of feelings as they appear to have existed even a hundred years back, some modification may I think be perceived to have taken place. Over the domestic and social intercourse of that time there seems to hang a certain kind of gloom which is certainly not characteristic of modern life. Whether or not this is the case, it is certain that social intercourse is attended with more or less cheerfulness as it is respectively surrounded or unsurrounded by enlightenment. The absence of a spirit of thought causes both the brighter and the more sombre personal feelings, to be realised less keenly. The joy of a comparatively unenlightened mind, is strong but not fine; and the sorrow, though it may fall upon stronger nerves, falls dead and without the recoil which a higher tempered mind tends to give it. On the other hand, if reflection tends to sober joy, it also helps to refine it; and if it should make sorrow more keenly felt it also renders it more hopeful. The development of new faculties of taste and appreciation, begets a

MUSICAL DEVELOPMENT. 139

keener and more versatile admiration; a refined and wide admiration tends to spiritualise, expand, and strengthen the feelings of love, friendship, and reverence; and the larger the capacity of the heart for these emotions the greater is its capacity for joy, and the more room it has for hope.

With the modification and development of the instinctive feelings has occurred a sympathetic change in their musical expression. This change is chiefly visible in that peculiar breadth and cheerfulness of spirit which distinguishes modern music inspired by natural feeling. As an example of breadth of spirit, I may mention a short composition entitled an 'Elegiac Song,' written by Beethoven, in memory of the wife of a friend, to words of which the general sense and spirit are conveyed in the following 'imitation' by Mr. Hullah :—' Sweet was thy presence; calm thy departure; too holy for regret. No tear should fall when a glorified spirit home returneth.' The music expresses the feelings of warm human love, sympathy with purity and virtue, constancy, keen but hopeful regret, and, in remarkable vividness, the brightness and glory of the heritage of religion. As an example

K 2

of cheerfulness of spirit, I may mention Haydn's setting of Shakespeare's lines, 'She never told her love.' Perhaps more sorrow could not be represented in so few words than is expressed in this passage. Yet the music is not gloomy; a warm atmosphere of charm surrounds the whole conception. The technical cause of this charm, may be found in those richer harmonious and melodic effects, and fresher musical idioms which it contains. These are the modern composer's materials; and they have become unfolded chiefly through that changed and more cheerful spirit which now animates emotion generally.

The influence of mental progress upon instrumental music is indicated in the works of Beethoven. I think it may be said that he accomplished his great works not simply because he possessed great genius and a thoughtful mind but because he also realised the great mental development characteristic of the time in which he lived, a period involving the end of the last and the beginning of the present centuries.

It would appear, then, that as both abstract and instinctive feelings are affected by enlightenment, the progress of music is sympathetically related to the general progress of the mind. It cannot be doubted that time exerts a beneficial influence upon every style of music, its tendency being to spiritualise and enrich. Each age has its art trivialities; and at times art may be principally represented by such works or by others which are but oft-repeated echoes from great works of the past. It is possible that the present may be such a time as this. Yet as the mind is growing and with it the heart, the source of all inspiration is widening; so that there is reason for awaiting patiently another advent of that combination of inordinate artistic and high moral capacity, called genius. An important consideration, however, is here suggested. I have remarked that scantiness of available resources for the production of effect, may have induced that technical discipline which resulted in the high development of the fugal art; and I have endeavoured to show that this art has influenced in an important way some of the greatest modern works. Now the present state of music, is the very opposite of that which led to this result. At the present time there is a plentifulness of resource, which time ever tends to increase; and it is possible that this circumstance may operate unfavorably upon composition. Another consideration here suggests itself. Inasmuch as under the influence of enlightenment the tendency of man's various emotions, is to unfold less independently of one-another, and to become so to speak each more all-inclusive; and since the expression of every feeling by art must therefore necessarily become broader, it would seem that the tendency of art-forms must be to approach one-another in spirit. We may thus expect that all separations of style which result from realising feeling in a partial way, will cease to exist; and that the different styles of music, like the variety of nature, will embrace more and more the spirit of the whole.

The reader will observe that the remarks which constitute this chapter, are both few in number and of a less practical character than the general matter of the work. They did not arise out of a deliberate intention to treat of the influence of mental progress upon music,—a subject which would bear far more lengthy consideration,—but occurred to me during the composition of the previous chapters; and I have thought it advisable to append them in this place. They, consequently, represent only a glance at the subject.

It is unnecessary for me to say that the aspect in which I have regarded music, demands a far deeper and more discursive examination than that which I have given to it. Oliver Wendell Holmes, referring to music, remarks :—'It has its seat in the region of sense rather than of thought. Yet it produces a continuous and, as it were, logical sequence of emotional and intellectual changes; but how different from trains of thought proper! how entirely beyond the reach of symbols!' The nature of the relation of these impressions; the reason why a couple or more notes arranged in a particular way, may express and imbue a certain phase of emotion, are considerations relating to a subject, doubtless extremely recondite, still, concerning which a mind qualified for its study might, perhaps, gain some knowledge. Is the emotional influence of a musical effect derived from our in the first place unconsciously associating its elements with those changes of sound that occur in verbal utterance? and does the vast impressiveness of music, thus, like other grand and complex influences are said to do, result from facts of experience combined with the influence of association?* That music on the one hand, and modulation and accent in speech on the other, are prompted by and appeal to, the same instinct, is all that I have ventured to assume; and on this standing-ground I have endeavoured to investigate the moral element of music. What this instinct is, and whether or not it has been developed from the use of language, are some of the many considerations relating to the subject, which I have passed over, yet which, doubtless, might be investigated with profit.

Apart from the special interests of music, the subject of its moral element is a highly important one in this respect: that it tends to raise considerations relating to that immaterial world with which all that is most serious in human life is concerned. Professor Bain, alluding to mental and bodily states, makes these remarks: 'Mental states and bodily states are utterly contrasted; they cannot be compared, they have nothing in common except the most general of all attributes, degree, and order in time. * * Walking

---

* See 'Dissertations and Discussions,' Vol. III., page 136. By J. S. Mill.

in the country in spring, our mind is occupied with the foliage, the bloom, and the grassy meads, all purely objective things : we are suddenly and strongly arrested by the odour of the May-blossom; we give way for a moment to the sensation of sweetness : for that moment the objective regards cease; we think of nothing extended; we are in a state where extension has no footing; there is, to us, place no longer. * * These subject-moments are studied to advantage in bursts of intense pleasure, or intense pain, in fits of engrossed reflection, especially reflection upon mental facts. * * When as in pure feeling—pleasure or pain—we change to the subject-attitude from the object-attitude, we have undergone a change not to be expressed by place; the fact is not properly described by the transition from the *external* to the *internal*, for that is still a change in the region of the extended. The only adequate expression is a *change of state :* a change from the state of the extended cognition to a state of unextended cognition. By various theologians, heaven has been spoken of as not a place, but a *state ;* and this is the only phrase that I can find suitable to describe the vast, though familiar and easy, transition from the material or extended, to the immaterial or unextended side of the universe of being.' If the being absorbed in that emotion of pleasure which high musical expression produces, may be classed among these subject-states, then music is a great, if it is not the greatest agent in producing them. Again music is the voice not only of those feelings which may be expressed by language but of much of that residue of feeling,—which probably constitutes the larger portion of emotional phenomena,—that lies behind all words. It would appear, then, that music is an important evidence of the immaterial world; and I think I may venture to say, that from its investigation by the regular student of moral science it is not improbable that there might accrue new knowledge of those spiritual states of life which contain our higher moments, as well as of the principles of one of the most efficient and exhaustive means of expression we possess.

For EU product safety concerns, contact us at Calle de José Abascal, 56–1°,
28003 Madrid, Spain or eugpsr@cambridge.org.

www.ingramcontent.com/pod-product-compliance
Ingram Content Group UK Ltd.
Pitfield, Milton Keynes, MK11 3LW, UK
UKHW041419180426
11947UKWH00007B/205